Tales of the Elders

Tales of the Elders

A Memory Book of Men and Women Who Came to America as Immigrants, 1900–1930

written and photographed by

Carol Ann Bales

MODERN CURRICULUM PRESS
Cleveland • Toronto

Modern Curriculum Press
A Division of Simon & Schuster
13900 Prospect Road
Cleveland, Ohio 44136

ISBN 0-8136-7215-5

1 2 3 4 5 6 7 8 9   96 95 94 93 92 91

Cover design by Antler & Baldwin, Inc.
Cover photograph/The Bettman Archive

For Pa,
Theodore W. Kothe

Contents

Acknowledgments

The author wishes to give special thanks to

Lorraine Martinez Holt, granddaughter of Natividad Gonzalez, who transcribed, with dispatch and a smile, nearly all of the
interviews.

Valerie McLenighan for the care and concern she has given to
this book as its editor.

Erma Perry, who suggested and interviewed Abe Gamberg
for me.

Donal Mahoney and Dolores Nathanson for their own
particular forms of nudging.

Jane Jewell, a friend who came to America from Scotland in
1929, for contributing to my understanding.

Bill McNair and Sylvia for their many years of help and
encouragement, which I needed.

All the friends, acquaintances, co-workers at the National
PTA, and representatives of organizations, especially Eve
Manzardo of Amalgamated Clothing Workers' Samuel Levin
Center for Retired Members, who suggested and contacted
persons to be interviewed.

And, finally, the twelve men and women included in this
book—and those interviewed but not included—for so gra-
ciously sharing their lives. This book is really their book.

"I don't know when anyone has asked me so many questions about past memories; tonight I feel so happy."
—Andrew Yiannapoulos,
following his conversation with the author

Introduction

Tales of the Elders is a collection of memories from the time of the Great Migration—a period between 1900 and 1930 when millions of immigrants came to America to work and many to make it their home.

Twelve men and women who made the journey during those years tell their stories in this book. Their recollections have been filtered through time; and while some may be exaggerated, others are understated. But each person has been honest and has considered this sharing of his or her life experiences to be important.

Their reminiscences are offered as illustrations of what the immigrant experience was like for some.

Although these twelve individuals came to America between 1900 and 1930, they were preceded by many others; immigration to this country has a long and complex history. It is a history shaped by events in other countries—by wars and revolutions, famines, persecution, and economic crises that motivated large numbers of people to seek a new and better life in America—and by the various immigration laws that were passed, repealed, revised, and amended in this country over the years.

The movement of immigrants to the United States began as a trickle in the early part of the nineteenth century. But by

1850, political turmoil in northern and western Europe, famine in Ireland, and an increasing demand for farmers and laborers to help build the expanding new nation had swelled the trickle to a torrent.

Before 1880, most immigrants came to America from northern and western Europe—from Britain, Ireland, Germany, Sweden, France, and the Netherlands—and from China. But by the turn of the century the pattern had changed. More immigrants began to arrive from southern and eastern Europe—from Italy, Greece, Austria, Russia, the Balkan countries—and from the Western Hemisphere, mainly from Canada and Mexico. This new wave of immigrants numbered as many as a million a year during the peak of the Great Migration.

Few limitations had ever been placed on immigration to this country, with two conspicuous exceptions: the Chinese Exclusion Act of 1882, which prevented the immigration of Chinese laborers, and the Gentlemen's Agreement of 1907 between Japan and the United States, which was designed to keep out Japanese laborers.

But the 1920s saw the passage of a new series of laws that limited the number of immigrants that might enter each year. These laws also set quotas that favored newcomers from the northern and western European countries. The result was a sharp drop in immigration between 1925 and 1929, when only 150,000 persons a year were allowed to enter.

These discriminatory laws were gradually replaced by new legislation providing for the equal treatment of everyone seeking entry to this country. Recently, some 400,000 persons a year have come to live in the United States, and they are more ethnically diverse than before 1965, when the national origins quota system set up in the 1920s was finally repealed. Immigration from Asian and southern European countries has increased; among America's most recent immigrants are some 125,000 Vietnamese refugees, many of whom are children.

History prevents us from including stories from all of this country's ethnic groups. Native Americans, for example, had already been living here for thousands of years before the first European immigrants arrived. Most black Americans now living are native-born, and the majority of their ancestors were forced to come to America in the days of the slave trade, long before the Great Migration. Few Orientals were able to enter the United States between 1900 and 1930 because of the discriminatory immigration laws in effect at the time.

The men and women whose recollections are printed in this book, then, represent only a few of America's many ethnic groups. They do not pretend to speak for their respective native lands or peoples. Their memories are of their own unique lives—all very personal, and therefore, very precious.

They tell of coming to America: what they left behind and why; how they made their way to the United States; what they hoped to find here; what they did find; and how they made new lives in this, a strange, new country.

1

It's a Nice Hat, But It's Not American

ABRAHAM GAMBERG *arrived in America at the age of nineteen. He didn't bring much—only a gift for the cousin who had lent him money to come, some clothing, and his father's respect for hard work and charitable giving.*

It was not much, it might seem, with which to start a new life in a new country—especially in a country whose language he couldn't speak. But Abe Gamberg had what he needed: his father's values and his own discipline and determination.

That was in 1913. Since then he has become one of Philadelphia's most successful and respected businessmen, a man honored many times for his work in charity and civic affairs.

At eighty-three, Abe Gamberg still works hard. He's up every morning by 4:00 A.M. and to work by 5:00 A.M., preparing to buy what amounts to millions of dollars' worth of meat each year for one of this country's largest food service management companies.

This is a man who gives his whole heart, not just to his work, but to everything he does. And he does everything; he is an exhibition dancer, a world traveler, an expert ice skater, and a cruise buff. For a time he was even Philadelphia's champion in horseback riding.

Abe Gamberg was born September 23, 1893, in the city of
Novozibkove in the Russian Ukraine. He was taught by a
rabbi, since Jews were not allowed to go to school in his city.
Abe says he is "crazy for education" and proud that his eight
grandchildren are all "college-bred people." Abe and his wife,
who is now dead, raised three children.

"You're neither young nor old; you're alive or dead," he has
said. Abraham Gamberg is very much alive.

I came to the United States on January 18, 1913, but I had
decided to leave Russia long before that. I was only eight or
nine years old when we had a *pogrom* in our city. Mobs of
Russians, non-Jewish people, robbed our stores; some Jewish people were killed. I hid in a cellar with my brother for
three days without food. I couldn't see that we had done
anything wrong to anybody—why should we be persecuted?
But it seems like Jews have always been scapegoats. At one
time I thought that Jewish people should be considered the
same as any other people, but they're not. Whatever happens
in a country—in Russia, or wherever—if people don't have
enough to eat, they seem to blame the Jews because the Jews
might own little stores.

I decided while I was still a child that I would leave such a
country. I thought, "The first chance I have, I'm going to go
away." And that's the chance that came to me when my
cousin sent me a paid passage to the United States.

I didn't really choose America to be my home. I came here
because I had my cousins here, and they sent me a passage.
Sixty bucks, what do you think? It wasn't cheap to come. Of
course, I had heard America was a great democracy—that

you didn't have to work twenty-four hours a day only to be persecuted, that everybody was equal, that people enjoyed freedom.

Before I left Russia, some people said about America: "All you have to do is to get a big shovel and a sack, and you go into the street and shovel the gold into the sack." But I wasn't a bit disappointed to find that you had to work for your living, because I was used to hard work. I was used to earning whatever I got; I always wanted to earn it.

I learned the meat business young, when I was only about six years old, because my father, grandfather, uncles—they were all in the meat business. In Russia in those days, if you were in the meat business, you had to be able to buy livestock, butcher it in the slaughterhouse, and do everything there was to be done to prepare the meat.

The first calf that I bought, I bought when I was only—I don't exactly remember, but I don't think I was over eight years of age. You see, where I come from in Russia, calves do not get born in wintertime. But one time when I was going to school, I saw a peasant with a sled, a wooden sled, taking a calf to the market. It was way below zero. So I went over to him and I said, "Uncle, how much do you want for the calf?"

Now, the Russian peasants were very joyful people, so he looks at me, a little fella like me, and he starts to laugh. "Do you want to buy the calf?"

I say, "Yeah!"

Then he says, "Well, how about the money?"

And I happen to have saved up some money that my mother and father had given me. I says, "Certainly, I got money; look at my pockets." And I showed it to him.

He says, "Well, how much you going to give me?"

"I'll give you all of it," I says. I had about two rubles, about two American dollars.

He says, "Okay, you got a calf."

He gave me a little rope, and I pulled the calf over to our town, to a certain section that was just meat markets. Every butcher came out running to see the miracle of a calf in January. And my older brother came up, and he says, "My God, where'd you get the calf?"

I says, "I bought it."

"Well, how much did you pay for it?" he says.

I says, "How much you going to give me for it?"

He says, "I'll give you five rubles."

That's a big profit, so I says, "Sold." That was my beginning.

Then, when I was not quite thirteen years old, my father had an accident and he died. His horse fell through the ice one day when he was on his way to market. And I had to take over. I started to buy for our two small meat shops. My mother was a pretty good butcher—she cut the meat. And I knew how to cut meat, too. But I always thought that I'm not going to stay in Russia because of the persecution.

Well, when I came to this country, my cousins picked me up at the railroad station in Philadelphia. I was sleepy because someone sold me in Jersey City a nice salami and candy. It was very delicious, and I ate so much that I fell asleep. I was very relaxed; I didn't have any fear about coming into a new country.

Anyway, I came here, and one of my cousins—I had two cousins—said to me, "Butcher business in this country is not good. I will take you to a factory where they produce overcoats, and you will become a presser—presser of over-coats."

I went, and I saw people sweating in that factory, horrible, even though it was cold outside. I says, "I couldn't do any kind of work like that."

And my cousin says, "Well, you can make money."

"I am a butcher," I says. "I can't do anything like that."

"Well," he says, "it's up to you."

So I went and got myself a job in a butcher shop. They gave me eight dollars a month plus room and board to work practically seven days and seven nights a week. The only time I had off was on Friday. I'd go to see my cousin, stay overnight there, and then in the morning I had to go back to work.

After I had been in this country for several months, I met a young man, and we became friendly. And he says to me, "Abe, I think we ought to get some education." I says, "Well, what are we going to do?" He says, "They have a night school in West Philadelphia High School. We can go at night. We can walk."

So, one winter evening—snow was knee-high—we walked from 59th and Market to 47th and Walnut, about fourteen blocks. We walked there after getting up at four in the morning to go to work, and I had worked pretty hard that day. I always gave everything I had to work; I didn't skimp, didn't do a half job. And neither did my friend. So we went to the school and we registered. We each put down a dollar. After working all day—and I had had a pretty good dinner, too—I sat down in the classroom. It was so nice and warm, and I remember the teacher started talking, and I just fell asleep. I fell asleep, and I started to snore something terrific.

Well, everybody laughed, and the teacher came over and shook me. Oh, I had a wonderful sleep. She woke me up, and she says, "Hey, boy, here's your dollar. Go home; you need the sleep better than education." And that was the beginning, or the end, of my formal education in this country.

I worked at my first job for only a short time. I found out that I could get another job in a storehouse in Camden, New Jersey, at five dollars a week. That was a terrific raise. I worked just a little while, and the woman—she was a widow running the storehouse—came to me, and she says, "Abram, I can't keep you here."

I say, "Why? Don't I do good work?"

She says, "You do too good a work. You're faster than all the other workers. And they say they'll go on strike if I keep you." So I was fired.

Then I found another job in Camden, in a butcher shop. But the guy I worked for over there woke me up at four in the morning to pray. I said, "I want to sleep yet." He says, "No, you gotta pray."

I worked there for about a week, and I said to myself, "I'm not going to stand for that." And I found myself a job in west Philadelphia to cut meat and deliver orders. And I was a success—I'll tell you why.

When I came to this country, I had a cap. My cousin, he says, "It's a nice cap, but it's not American." He says, "I'll buy you a derby hat." And he says, "I'll buy you a new red suit for eight dollars—a burlap suit with a celluloid collar. That's American." And he buys me new red shoes. "That's American," he says.

So, in this outfit, I started taking orders and making deliveries for the butcher in west Philadelphia. The first

20

customer I had was at 5532 Locust Street. I'll never forget that address. I had a lot of trouble finding it because we didn't have street numbers in my city in Russia. I guess the bell didn't work, so I opened the door and walked in. There were about five or six women playing bridge. Well, they took one look at me in my red suit, red shoes, and derby hat, and became hysterical with laughter. I says, I'm the butcher, and I work for so and so on 59th and Market, and I'd like to get an order for the next day. In Jewish, they could hardly understand me, and they were dying from laughing to see such a character. But I got the order. People enjoyed my outfit so much that they'd buy from me. And in three months I got my boss 160 new accounts.

First he gave me a pushcart to deliver the meat; then I was promoted, and he got me a bicycle. I said, "We gotta have some help—160 new customers." So we hired one man with a pushcart and another man with a bicycle, and I got a horse and wagon. I was raised to ten dollars a week. And from then on it was very easy for me.

The business grew so much that I said to my boss, "Look, there's a need for a butcher shop on 53rd Street. I tell you what we do: Let's go into business together. You and I will be partners, only you be the boss. I work for you, but whatever profit there is in that store, you give me ten dollars of it first for my salary, and whatever is left over in profit, we'll split." But his wife said, "No, Sam—no partners, no partners."

So I said, "Well, if you don't want partners, you don't want to go into partnership. Either way, whatever we make, we split."

He said, "No, Molly said no." Molly wore the pants; she was tough. Maybe too tough.

So I said, "Here's two weeks' notice—I'm going to leave you. Get yourself another man because I'm going to open up a store."

And I did open up the store. Little by little, I started to do really good. People flocked into my store because I was an expert in meat. They stayed in line to buy meat off me. And that is part of the story of my beginning in business. I didn't do badly.

When I had saved up enough money, I brought my sister over from Russia, then my brother. And later my wife's family. I also loaned money to a cousin to come to this country. And I sent money to my mother in Russia.

I had a very beautiful mother, not because she was my mother, but looking at her as a person. She had an angelic face. When I see the *Mona Lisa*, it reminds me a great deal of her. She was not educated—she couldn't read or write—but she had a good heart and a good mind. A wonderful mother.

I remember when she took me to the railroad station to go to America. I sat down in the train, and I wondered if I'd ever see her again. I can still feel tears. The tears come out of my eyes right now. My heart is full. I never saw my wonderful mother again. I tried to get her to come over to this country, but she wouldn't come because she had grandchildren in Russia. My brother left a lot of children, and my mother said, "My life belongs to them." She was a very dedicated person. No, not dedicated—she felt it was her responsibility.

The only things I brought from Russia were myself and the values of my mother and father. I am what my father was—his philosophy. He was a very religious man, not because he went to synagogue three times a day, but because he lived religiously. Each of us children had a little box, and if we had five cents, we put one penny into that box for charity. We were to give to others even if it meant to deny ourselves.

In that little town in Russia, we didn't have running water. We drew our water from a common well. And when you went there early in the morning, you'd always find something beside the well. It might be a chicken, a couple of eggs, a loaf of bread, or a cake. No one ever knew who gave it. But the person who really needed the food took it; the person who didn't need it wouldn't take it. That's what I call charity.

I'm still working every day, and most of my paycheck goes to people who need it. My accountant says, "My God, you got more charities on your list than anybody that I know." I give to the poor, the blind, the crippled; to Catholic Charities, the Red Cross; and, of course, I'm very interested in Jewish people.

I like to give, to be charitable—just like my father. I can't get away from my father's thoughts and beliefs because he was a truthful person and made such an impression on me that if I live to be a thousand, I'll never want to be any different from my father.

2

A Baby Is Born in a Boxcar

Natividad Martinez Gonzalez *was born in Lardo, a village in the state of Durango, Mexico, on Christmas Day, 1907. In celebration, she was named Natividad, which means "Christmas" in Spanish.*

She grew up during the Revolution of 1910 in Mexico. At that time wealthy landlords owned huge estates, while the majority of Mexicans, the peasants, remained in poverty. The Revolution sought social justice and economic progress for all Mexicans. It was a violent time, a time when people of all classes joined revolutionary bands led by heroes such as Francisco "Pancho" Villa, Emiliano Zapata, General Victoriano Huerta, and Venustiano Carranza.

These revolutionary bands rode through the Mexican countryside attacking federal troops, sometimes looting and terrorizing towns and estates, destroying railroads—and fighting one another. When the Revolution finally ended, Mexico adopted a new constitution, which brought about many reforms.

But in the meantime, the violence had made life difficult in Mexico. It was to escape this aspect of the Revolution that Natividad's father brought his family to the United States in 1918 while he worked on the Santa Fe Railroad.

I remember my mother's house in Durango, Mexico, when I was a child. It was really beautiful. It was a big house. And it had those marble floors with black and white squares, and a veranda with fancy ironwork. It was a house that belonged to rich people who had fled during the Revolution. They rented it to my mother. All of us children—we were five sisters and one brother—slept in one big room, and my mother and father slept in another room. The house had a big, big kitchen and a big table. Those rich people must have had a lot of company because they had such a big table. And they had a stable that my mother rented out. But what I remember the most is a big stone trough that was always filled with water for the horses. I liked to go in and take a bath because the water was so cool. The trough was stone—like marble—and every day I went in.

I remember, too, going with my mother to wash our clothing; we walked to a stream with a lot of stones very far from our house. I remember my mother washing our clothes on the stones by that running stream, and all the other women washing. They took our clothing off to wash it and then gave us a bath. When we came back, everything was clean.

My parents weren't rich, but they made a living. My mother had a fruit stand. She sold Mexican ice cream—something like sherbet—and whatever fruits were in season. She bought the fruits in another town. My father made candy, all kinds of Mexican candy: milk candy, coconut candy, sweet potato candy, watermelon candy. He made it in our house, and I remember big pails of candy sitting around. They put me to rolling it out sometimes, and if I went too slow, they'd slap my hands.

If it hadn't been for the Revolution, I think we'd still be

living there. All my children would have been born in Mexico. I remember the Revolution. It was really bad. When the troops came into the towns, there was shooting all over and looting. One time I was playing in the yard, and I heard a lot of shooting, and my mother was so afraid. "Come in, come in," she said. Our town was a little town—I don't think it was even five blocks around—but when they came through, they grabbed whatever they could. When men like that have guns, they can do whatever they want. My father couldn't work anymore making the candy because no one bought candy. The people were afraid to go out of their houses.

But mostly I remember my mother crying, "I don't want my boy going to the Revolution." She was afraid for my brother, who was seventeen. You see, when the soldiers came into the towns, they took the young boys twelve years old and up with them. They took them to repair railroad lines and do things like that. But then, little by little, they gave them guns and taught them to fight.

I remember one time when Pancho Villa came into our town, everyone was saying, "Villa is coming, Villa is coming." They were glad because they knew they would have something to eat when he came. Pancho Villa was a revolutionary leader, but he was more for the common people than the others. They said he opened up railroad boxcars filled with corn, and the people came and took what they needed. He took from the rich, but he gave to the poor.

I can still hear my mother crying and saying, "I don't want to stay here." And I knew it was because of my brother. She was worried about him. And so, well, she had a lady friend living in Juarez near the border, the Mexico-United States border, and this friend wrote, "Why don't you come here?" She said a lot of people were passing from Juarez to El Paso, Texas—just on the other side of the border—to work.

And that's how it happened that we all went to Juarez. My father and my brother passed into the United States to look for jobs while the rest of us stayed in Juarez with my mother. They registered for a job at the railroad agency in El Paso—it was like an employment agency for railroad work—and got a contract to work six months on the Santa Fe Railroad in Kansas. And in 1918 my father brought us all into the United States. I've stayed here ever since; I never went back, except for a visit.

When I came to the United States, I remember once we went to a restaurant, but they wouldn't let us go in because we were Mexicans. They said to my father, "Take the food out onto the street." I remember I asked why they didn't let us go in—all the other people were eating inside. Why didn't they let us go in, too?

I think that was the first time that we went out to eat in this country, and I don't remember that we ever went out again. My father was disappointed, you know, and he didn't take us out anymore because he didn't want us to be treated like that. He was a very proud person. He would never take nothing from nobody. He knew how to treat people. In Mexico he owned his own business, but he never treated his workers badly.

While my father and my brother worked building branch lines for the Santa Fe Railroad in Kansas, we lived in boxcars in a moving camp. The boxcar was like one big room, with a kitchen at one end and a bedroom at the other. The kitchen had a wood stove, a table and chairs, and a cabinet. The boxcar had sliding doors on either side and a couple of windows. Well, it was nice in a way, but it was just a plain railroad car. It wasn't plastered or anything on the inside. The company gave us the boxcar to live in—we didn't have to pay rent for it. They gave each family a boxcar. Sometimes there were twenty boxcars with twenty families living in one long line, all families from Mexico.

Whenever the work was done on one section of the railroad, the engine came to pull us to another section. My mother used to keep the tub and all the facilities for washing down under the boxcar. And when the camp was going to move, they'd tell the people, "Everything you got on the bottom, put up, because the camp is going to move."

I remember we children were always glad when they moved the camp. But sometimes they moved us at night while we were asleep, and we didn't even know.

They'd build a little branch track alongside the main line, and that's where they put the camp. It was usually in the country near some farms, and we'd go to buy milk, eggs, and whatever they had on the farms. We bought most of our groceries in camp, though. One boxcar was a grocery store. And our water came from a water tank pulled along with the boxcars.

My father worked for about two years building different sections of the Santa Fe Railroad, and we moved from camp to camp. One camp, I remember, was in Hanston, Kansas, and another one was in Florence, Kansas, and another in White City, Kansas. Then we stopped at El Dorado, Kansas, and we lived in a company house in a little Mexican settlement. And when my father worked in Tiresville, Kansas, we lived in tents in a tent camp. We stayed there all summer. My mother cooked meals for all the camp people, and we had to help her with the work. But at most of the camps, only my father and my brother worked. We played. We were always running and picking wild flowers, and my mother taught me to read and write in Spanish.

I never went to school because we were always moving, and moving, and moving, and nowhere near a town. And there was no teacher to come to the camp to teach the children. I started first grade in El Paso, and again in El Dorado when we lived in the settlement. But I was already a teenager, and then I got married and had my babies. I think I could be smart because all my papers had 100 on them, but I never had a chance to learn.

When my children started school, they taught me to speak English. But it was hard for them, too. They didn't know English either when they first started to school, and their teacher said, "Tell your mother to speak English." But they learned, and they tried very hard to teach me.

You know, I was so young when I got married—only fourteen and a half. My husband came from a town just across the river from my hometown in Mexico, but we met in this country. We eloped. You see, my father wanted to go back to Mexico so bad. He wasn't used to common labor, like on the railroad, because he always had his own business in Mexico. And he wanted to go back to start a business again. But I didn't want to go back—I remembered living in Juarez. First we lived with another family, and then my mother rented a little house, and all the water was coming in when it rained. And I was sleeping on the floor. I didn't like it. I said, "I'm not going to Mexico no more." I think that's why I ran away to get married: I didn't want to go back to Mexico. We were married in a church and everything, and my brother stayed to see me married. Then he went back to Mexico with my parents. That was in 1921, but my father died the next year with a heart attack. And my brother brought the family back, and we were reunited again in Kansas.

When I got married, you know, we had it pretty hard. All the time that I was pregnant with my first baby, my husband had no job, and we were living with my father's uncle. But then my husband got a job again with the railroad, and we were living in a boxcar camp in Merriam, Kansas. That's where I had my first baby—in a boxcar in Merriam, Kansas. I had eight babies all together, but three of them died. Three of my babies were born in Kansas City, Missouri, where my husband was working in a packinghouse. The rest of my children were born in Chicago. In 1926 we moved to Chicago, where we've lived ever since, and my husband worked in packinghouses until he retired.

When we came to Chicago, it was during the depression, and we were poor. But someone must have written something about us in the *Tribune.* Anyway, when my first baby boy was born, I received baskets of baby clothes and a chicken with all the trimmings. It happened at that time that my sister stayed with me for ten days and sewed clothing for my children. Well, we lived on the first floor, and someone opened the window, came in, and took everything—the new baby clothes and the clothes my sister had made. But that was the depression.

Now people say they're going to move because the schools are no good, the neighborhood is no good. But at that time, when my children were small, we lived in the gangsters' neighborhood—in Capone's neighborhood. It was terrible. But nothing happened to us, except the stolen clothes.

We had some hard times in this country, but I always had my family with me. My husband saw to it that I was near my mother. He never had a family; his family had died. He knew what a family meant. Even after we were all married, my sisters and I, we always lived only one or two blocks away from my mother. We were one family together. My brother lives upstairs from us now.

Nowadays, the girl gets married and goes to the suburbs. I have five children: two girls in the suburbs, one girl in the state of Arizona, and two boys in the suburbs. All so far away from us. But if we want to visit them, they come to pick us up. It's a pretty big crowd when we all get together. We have five children, fourteen grandchildren, and ten great-grandchildren. My husband says we are blessed to live to see so many "little roots" take hold and grow.

3

A Single Thought: Get to America

When he landed in Hoboken, New Jersey, GEORGE THIEL was a young man eager to start a new life. Born in Amsterdam in 1898, he had left the Netherlands to come to the United States in 1919, soon after World War I had ended. He had the address of a fellow Hollander, the nephew of a friend of his father, who owned a dairy farm in Michigan. But he didn't have enough money to get there.

Propped up in a chair in the empty lobby of a hotel, George spent his first night in this country thinking about his future. The drive "just to get to America," to leave behind the wars and misery of Europe, had been strong—so strong that he hadn't even considered what he might do once he arrived.

It took him nearly a month to work his way across the country to the Michigan dairy farm. He stayed there to help for several months before going to work on a bulb farm in a nearby town. In the years since, George has worked as a salesman for a wholesale seed company in Sedalia, Missouri, as a construction supervisor for a real estate firm in Chicago, and as the chief steward at the Edgewater Beach Hotel in Chicago. Now in his late seventies, George says he tried retirement for one year when he was sixty-five, but it just didn't work out; he went back to work full-time for a real estate firm.

George Thiel and his wife, Katie, live in an apartment building on Chicago's North Side. They have one son; he is married and has several children. Although George regrets that it is difficult to make friends with younger people, he and his wife are very young in spirit and outlook. Humor crackles between the two—with George playing straight man. One trace of George Thiel's heritage is ever present: his Dutch "Schimmelpenninck" cigars. He has been buying them at the same cigar shop in Chicago for the past thirty years.

At the outbreak of the First World War, I went with a school friend to visit a small German town just on the other side of the Holland border. We were boys about sixteen years of age. On one particular day, August 1, 1914, we went to look at a blast furnace in a steel factory just outside of town. But when we got back to the boardinghouse where we had rented a room, we were told in no uncertain terms that we had to leave the country within twelve hours, or we would be arrested as spies. We purposely neglected to take the so-called last train to Holland because we had decided to bicycle our way back to Holland over country roads.

But before we started back, my friend wanted to pick up a letter from his mother at the post office. He was a mama's boy. It was all right that we had gone on a vacation to a far-off country, but he had to write a letter every couple of days to Mama, and Mama faithfully answered his letters. Thank goodness we had our bicycles. You couldn't get on a streetcar; you couldn't get on a bus. Both the army and navy were mobilizing. Germany had declared war on Russia that day. People were wild. Men were dashing home to change into their brand-new uniforms, the so-called field gray. Our landlady, everybody, was in an uproar—not necessarily in a bad mood, but certainly opposed to anything foreign.

The traffic was so heavy with bicycles, carriages, and a few automobiles that my friend went on into the post office, and I agreed to wait on the sidewalk across the street. I couldn't do much but walk up and down and keep constantly watching the entrance. And then, all of a sudden, the almighty policeman stopped traffic and disappeared across the street. Next thing I knew, crossing the street with the policeman in tow came a typical Prussian, militaristic German army officer, all dolled up in a brand-new wide cape and with the typical monocle in his eye. Everybody, including myself, was watching this scene intently. And this guy, as I watched, came steering straight toward me.

I just stood there looking at him. He came up to me, and in a most military voice he crackled, "What are you doing here?"

"I'm waiting for my friend," I said.

"Where is he?"

"In the post office."

And the policeman, wanting to put his nickel's worth in, said, "Answer all questions truthfully."

"I have no reason to do otherwise," I said.

The German army officer repeated, "What are you waiting for?"

"I told you—my friend in the post office."

"What is he doing there?"

"Getting a letter from his mother."

And then he says, "What are you staring at me for? I saw you walking up and down, and you kept looking at me."

I said, "I'm sorry, but if I looked at you, it must have been in admiration of your new uniform."

He told the policeman to watch and see if I was telling the truth, then left. Thank goodness, in a minute or two my friend came out with a letter in his hand. Then the policeman gave us some fatherly advice: "You boys had better get out of here."

I wanted to tell you that story because it symbolizes to me the typical overbearing attitude of the military clique in Germany before World War I. Everything and everybody was scared stiff of a guy with a uniform on. See what I mean?

Well, we pedaled our way toward the border and a small triangle of land between Holland, Germany, and Belgium, probably no more than a square mile, which we had learned in school happened to be a neutral area respected by all countries throughout the years. We parked ourselves for the night in this neutral area. It was hilly, and our spot was a little higher than the surrounding roads. Before the sun rose, we saw streams and streams of military coming from Germany over the adjoining country roads going into Belgium.

It was the German invasion of Belgium that started World War I. It would seem primitive today—those horses and marching men. And we saw the biggest, most famous cannon of the war—Big Bertha, the 98-ton howitzer used a few days later to shell the cities of Belgium.

The officer of one group turned his horse toward us and galloped up the little hill. He wanted to know what we were doing there. We told him that we were on our way to Holland and, trying to the best of our ability not to offend him, explained that we felt as long as we were located on that neutral hill adjoining Holland, he should keep on going and leave us alone.

My four older brothers and I were all nationalistic, but we had a hatred of wars and militarism. At different intervals, starting in 1908, my brothers left Holland to escape the wars of Europe. They went to all parts of the world. The oldest one went to Africa; the second oldest went to Rumania and then to the Dutch East Indies; the other two both went to Australia. So there are branches of the Amsterdam Thiel family in all parts of the world. But I was the youngest, and I got caught up in the war—World War I. I was in the army from 1917 to 1918—right up to November 11 at eleven o'clock, the eleventh day of the eleventh month in 1918, when the war ended.

I'll tell you one story about the war. We're talking now about November 9, 1918, in Holland, at the southernmost tip of the province of Limburg, where I was stationed. There had been numerous border incidents between Belgians and Germans during the previous four years. At this particular time the railroad tracks, which hadn't been used for four years, were overgrown with weeds. But at about five o'clock in the morning a train approached with full lights.

Our nearest outpost, very close to the border, was a man in a sod hut. He waved his flag and red lantern, and the train stopped. He was asked by a German army officer on the train if a higher authority might be found nearby. The Hollander said he would try to locate someone, but in the meantime, the train should stay where it was.

The Dutch soldier then pedaled his bicycle a mile and a half to where I and five others were stationed. We sent four soldiers back with him to make certain the train did not move, and I went on a bicycle to the nearest town to tell our lieutenant and a captain about the incident. Eventually our lieutenant was told that the train contained the German kaiser, Wilhelm II, and his entourage.

The kaiser had abdicated and was seeking political asylum in Holland. He and his entourage appeared to be in good living circumstances, although all the sleeping cars had their curtains drawn. I don't know the details from that point on, but I do know that the Holland government decided to intern the kaiser and that he was allowed to go to live in Holland at a castle belonging to a friend.

While we were in the army, occasionally we got a rest period, and I, of course, would try to go to Amsterdam to visit my father. Holland was badly in need of food. Whatever meat was available went to the army. It was ground up into sausage. At first those pieces of sausage, which were issued out to us regularly, measured about an inch-and-a-half thick and maybe twelve inches long; but as the war continued, the sausages got shorter and shorter. I knew the situation for my father at home—no meat. And so I saved from my issues all the sausages I could, and I carried them home. I had to carry the sausages on me, or they would have been stolen. We had quite a feast between the two of us, my father and I, on a few potatoes and my unique sausage.

By the end of the war my father was still living, but my mother had died—I missed her a great deal—and my brothers had all gone in different directions. I looked around, and as far as I could see, there wasn't much future in Europe for a young fellow. I decided the United States would be far enough away from the militarism of Europe that I might have a better chance to make a living.

I told my father, "As soon as I can, I want to go to the United States." Well, that was a little bit hard on him, I guess, but he was sensible enough to realize that in Holland there was no immediate future for me. He had lost everything in his business, and so on. But I discovered that I had to have someone to go to in the United States, or they wouldn't give me a visa. My father had had a very good friend—they called one another brothers—and this good friend had adopted a nephew, who had later emigrated to the United States. He had a farm in Michigan. We wrote to this nephew, and he agreed to sponsor me.

I was so eager to get out of Holland and go to the United States that that was all I could think about. Due to my military experience, I was able to get a job as a customs-immigration officer on the Holland-Germany border, and after a couple of weeks' training, I made big money—big money for me. And pretty soon I had saved enough for the trip.

I packed one of those big suitcases and a little hand-case, and that was all I took. I got on the ship—that was in January 1919—and I had a wonderful time. Plenty of good food and nothing to do for fourteen days. We had a ball. It was just wonderful. And, of course, we made girl friends, and the girls made boyfriends. Drinks were flowing—beer and wine. A person could really forget all the troubles of the war.

The passengers were all nationalities—except Germans and Austrians that had participated in World War I, just past. The people on the ship were leaving the hunger and destruction in Europe caused by the war. They came from the Balkan states, from Belgium, from France, and from Holland.

In the third-class cabins next to mine were a lot of women from Balkan countries. They had managed to scrape enough money together to get passage to the United States, but some of them didn't have visas, and they couldn't speak a word of any language but their own. Probably because of their recent experience of hunger, they insisted that every meal be brought to their cabins. But a half hour later, the stewards would have to come back to clean up because the women couldn't take the food; it made them sick. That went on for fourteen days. All the windows had to be kept closed because of stormy weather, and you can imagine the smell as you went past those cabins. But I never lost my appetite. I stayed on the upper decks.

We had left with 1,300 passengers, and when we arrived in Hoboken, we had 1,306 passengers—six babies were born on the trip. So we landed in Hoboken on a Saturday night, and it was raining like nobody's business. And then came the formalities of the passport and your visa. I had no problem with that; everything was in order, and I didn't fear it. But you had to have $125 or the equivalent to enter the United States in those days. I had started with $100, but after what I spent on the ship in those fourteen days, I had only $25 left. The immigration officer, after he saw that my passport was okay and that the board of health person had looked into my eyes and at my tongue, asked me about money. He says, "You got $125?"

"Yeah," I says, "it's all buttoned up inside my pocket here."

"You got it?" he says.

I says, "Yeah."

"Okay, go on," he says. That was my biggest relief!

I went off that gangplank onto the street in Hoboken. And by the poor gaslight I could see cabs, hacks as they called them, and guys wanting to carry your baggage. They were all hollering, and I couldn't understand half of what they were hollering about. I looked up the street at those cobblestones reflecting the gaslight, and I thought, "Now that you're here, what in the heck are you going to do?" And that was the first time the question had entered my brain. Before that moment, the only thing I could think about was just to get to the United States.

I saw a poorly lit sign: Hotel for Men. I walked in, and the fella that ran the place, a Jewish fella who talked a little German, says, "You come off the ship?"

"Yeah," I said.

And he had a room that cost thirty-five cents a night. I asked him if I could pay for three nights in advance and get a lower rate. He says, "Well, I know how it is; give me a dollar." So I saved a nickel.

I got a bed, and it was clean. I didn't know what to do with myself, but I spotted some comfortable chairs at street level in front of some big windows in the lobby. I sat down on one of those chairs and started to think.

There wasn't much doing on a Saturday night, and pretty soon the manager came over and started a conversation. He asked where I wanted to go. I said, well, I couldn't go anywhere until I had made some money. He told me that he had a friend who owned a hardware store just down the street. There had been a fire, and maybe he could use some help.

So the next morning I found the burned-out hardware store. I talked in German, and the owner talked in his German-Yiddish, and we got to understand each other. He could use some help. In those days nails of all sizes came in wooden kegs, and due to the fire, the wooden kegs had been burned, leaving the nails scattered about. So I got the job of sorting out nails in a burned-out hardware store. I forgot what he paid me, but he always brought me a nice pickle sandwich with some sausage on it for lunch.

I stayed with him for two or three weeks. I had, in the meantime, found out how much it would cost me to go to Michigan to the man who had sponsored me. Well, my money would only go as far as Buffalo, New York, on the Delaware and Lackawanna Railroad. So I said goodbye to my Jewish friend, and I got a train ticket to Buffalo. In Buffalo I looked around a little bit and discovered a great big restaurant, where I got a job as sort of a food regulator. I stayed there about ten days and picked up enough money to get to Chicago. I didn't like Chicago at all. I had some money, but not enough to go to Coloma, Michigan. So I went to the Travelers Aid Society, and they staked me to a little extra money.

I finally got off the train around five or six o'clock in the evening in Coloma—three or four weeks after I arrived in the United States. It had taken me that long to work my way from New York to Michigan. Coloma was a little village, not many stores, but I did see a hotel for men. I made the fellow at the hotel understand who I wanted to go to. He managed to reach these people by telephone, although it was a party line with six or eight people on the line. The man said it was too late for him to pick me up—too dark and too far—but that he'd come pick me up in the morning.

So the next morning, here he came with a team of horses and an open wagon. He had to get feed for his dairy cattle and pick up some groceries, and then we juggled off. And I never was so cold in my life. We had a horse blanket over our knees and bricks beside us that had been heated before we left. And that's the way we traveled over the six miles to his farm.

This man had a wife and a young child about a year old. Oh, the house was huge—thirteen rooms, a frame house. And cold. Outside, I remember a windmill that pumped the water, and when the wind blew it squeaked like the dickens because it was not greased. He had a herd of twenty-five or thirty purebred Holstein cows, and I learned a lot in those days about a dairy farm.

I got acquainted with the neighbors half a mile away and found out that we could make some extra money cutting trees in a nearby woods—sassafras trees. They had to be only two inches in diameter and eighteen inches long. We put them in cords four feet high and six feet long. We made $1.25 and had to split it between the three of us—my neighbor, the friend I was staying with, and myself. But do you know who bought that wood? The Ford automobile company in Detroit. It was used to make steering wheels on the Model T car.

I stayed on the dairy farm in Michigan until May of that year. But there wasn't much to do, no young people. I saw an ad in a magazine, *Florist Review:* Help wanted at a bulb farm in the little town of Eau Claire, Michigan. I went over there on horseback—twenty miles, a long distance in those days.

They gave me a job. It turned out that five other boys from Holland were working on this bulb farm, and it was run by a man from Holland. Well, that was pretty good. And we had excellent food, a room, and I forgot what we made, but it was big money—twenty-five or thirty dollars a week. And we were all in the same boat: They were recent immigrants who'd come to the United States for the same reasons that I had come.

We all had some trouble with the English language, and somehow we heard about a schoolteacher in town. We approached her, and she agreed to teach us English and to prepare us to take the examination for our high school diplomas. I had graduated from a horticultural college in Holland; I had received an education. But my English was a stumbling block. We went three times a week to the farmhouse where she boarded. She was a girl of about nineteen. We had a lot of fun. But she did manage to pump enough into us that we were able to pass the examination. So my high school diploma comes from the little town of Dowagiac, Michigan.

After that, I worked for a wholesale seed merchant in Sedalia, Missouri, and had many adventures. But about seven years after I had come to the United States, I decided to go back to Holland for a visit. And thus began the greatest adventure of my life: I met my wife, Katie.

4

Where Are the Cowboys, George?

KATIE KAMP THIEL *was born in the small German town of Meppen in 1907. She remembers the times of hunger and deprivation she suffered as a young girl growing up in Germany during World War I, and she remembers her family being divided by war and militarism. She says she "got her nose full" of those things in Europe, was happy to leave, and never wished to return for more than a visit.*

George Thiel had just returned to Europe from the United States for a visit when Katie met him in 1926. She was then working in the Netherlands as a hotel maid in The Hague. She sent an enthusiastic letter about George to her mother, who ordered Katie to come home immediately. Mrs. Kamp was apprehensive; two of her daughter's previous letters had told about an American couple who wished to take Katie to the United States as their adopted daughter and about a young man in the company of King Faisal who wished to take Katie to Saudi Arabia as a bride.

Katie followed her mother's orders and returned home, but she took George with her. When Mrs. Kamp saw that this time her daughter was serious, she approved of the marriage. George and Katie were then wed in Meppen by a young minister performing his first wedding ceremony.

*George returned to the United States in March 1926, and
Katie followed several months later. "I never had it so good in
my life as I had it on the boat," Katie says. "Oh, my gosh, you
got service and your meals. It was wonderful!"*

*For many years Katie and a friend operated a beauty shop on
Chicago's South Side, but she had to give up the partnership
when she and George moved to the North Side. After the move,
while George worked at the Edgewater Beach Hotel, Katie
opened a nursing home. She is proud of what she calls the
home's "Swedish smorgasbord" quality—that it was open to
people of all races and religious beliefs. She ran the home for
nine years. Because she was able to work and to help people,
Katie recalls that period as a satisfying time in her life.*

When I arrived in America, I thought this was a wonderful
country, even during the depression. You know, in Europe
we knew only hunger and wars. I remember when I was a
little girl in my hometown of Meppen, Germany, after the
First World War. We were starving; we had nothing to eat.
You've seen pictures of children with great big stomachs from
starvation? I was like that. A slice of turnip—that was our
sandwich. We used to beg for food from the farmers. Oh, my
God, that was terrible.

But in our little town was a prisoner of war camp for French
soldiers. The French prisoners got their packages from
France at nine o'clock in the morning. And we kids knew
that. We used to go and stand outside the wire fence, and the
French soldiers would pass food to us through the fence. Ya,
they did that. They used to get white bread from their
mothers; we thought it was cake. When I was living in
America, I wrote to de Gaulle, the French president. I told

him, "I will never forget what your soldiers did for us starving children. I love the French, and I will never forget." I wrote that to him.

And, you know, we were brought up at home with the kaiser. With my papa it was the kaiser this, the kaiser that. You've heard of the Battle of Jutland in the Skagerrak Strait? It was the largest naval battle of World War I; more than 8,000 people were killed. My oldest brother, Hans, was in that battle. He was George's age. A navy officer, a big shot in the navy. He came home—he was a handsome one with all his medals—and he says to my father, "Daddy, what did you tell us all those years about the kaiser? I'm finished with all that; no more killing for me! I will never give no more orders of killing and that's the end of that."

And my father—he was a good man, don't get me wrong—he slapped my brother's face. He said, "Don't talk about the kaiser like that to me." And my oldest brother disappeared. He was so hurt that my daddy had gotten so stern with him over the kaiser business that he went away. We never heard from him again.

We should learn from our experiences that wars are wrong, don't you think? Killing is terrible. Look at Vietnam, the people we killed over there. Isn't that pitiful? The poor women and children, I feel so sorry for them. And for what? I don't care what face it is, yellow or white; for me they're human beings. George and I don't like war. But still George says that if another country, right or wrong, ever actually attempted to invade this country, he would go out tomorrow and help in whatever way he could to chase them out.

I was working in a hotel in The Hague—it was 1926—when I met George. My sister calls me and says, "Katie, I'm going to have a party. Will you come and bring a girl friend? There are two fellows here that need dates." Well, the two fellows were George, who'd come from America, and his cousin from the Dutch East Indies.

George and I stuck together that whole evening, and we had a nice time. When they took me to the train to go back to The Hague, what did he do, that quiet man? He bought a ticket to go to The Hague, too. He stayed the whole week in The Hague. See what I mean? Quiet, but make sure.

Then he began to talk, "I like you. I want to marry you. Oh, marry me!" He asked would I like to go to America. America? My goodness, the cowboys are in America! You know, as a child I had read about cowboys in the magazines.

"That's where I'm going," I said. But first I had to ask my mommy. So I wrote to my mommy, and she said, "Katie, you come home right away; I never met that man."

I told George he'd have to go home with me to meet my mother. So we went to Germany to my little hometown, and my mommy looked at him, and she said, "He's a nice man." So we got together. George is very quiet; I'm just the opposite. We were married in Germany, and George went back to the United States. I came later.

The boat landed in New York, and I saw the Statue of Liberty and all the high-rises. I said, "George, is this America? Where are the cowboys?"

"Oh, pipe down," he says, "you'll see the cowboys some-day."

It was how many years later?—twenty-seven years later—that we finally took a trip west, and I saw cowboys. See, you get big ideas about cowboys when you're a kid. I thought America was full of cowboys.

We visited my great-uncle's grave in California on that trip. My great uncle—his name was Herman Hoormann—came to America in about 1840 and went in a covered wagon to San Francisco. He found gold. And in about 1890 he went back to Europe to visit my mommy. He wanted to open a butcher shop in San Francisco for my father, who was a butcher. But my father thought, just like I did, that America was such a wild country. And Papa was so quiet. So my Uncle Herman went back to America alone. But I often wished my father had decided to go to America, too.

When we visited San Francisco, we found that my uncle had owned land and buildings on Taylor and Van Ness streets. He must have been a very wealthy man. I said to George, "I want to go over there once and see where that great-uncle of mine was buried." I thought, oh, maybe under a little cross. You should have seen the great big monument! It was as high as the ceiling. Herman Hoormann, born in Meppen, Germany. I stood there and thought, "You should know that your grandniece stands here. She came to America, too."

I forgot to tell you—before I came to America, when I was the only child left at home, I went to visit my father in the hospital. He said to me, "Katie, take care of Mommy if I'm gone." I said I would do that.

So before we got married, I told George, "You know, I can't go to America because I promised my papa I'd take care of Mama."

"Oh, don't you worry about that," George said. "Your mama can come to us in America."

Two years later, Mama was all alone in Europe. Her eight children had all disappeared—one here, one there. And we wrote, "Mama, would you like to come visit us?" She said she'd love it. We sent her a ticket and got her a visa for six months. You know how long she stayed? Nine years.

And if I had it to do over again, I would do it tomorrow. She was so happy here in this country. You know, she had been through all that mess in Europe—the wars and Papa's sickness and inflation in Germany. For a thousand dollars you couldn't even buy a pound of butter, ya. And then Mommy came here, and, boy, she had the life of a queen. You know, going out with the women's clubs, having luncheons downtown. She had it nice.

But then, just before the Second World War, she was worried about my brothers and sisters. She said, "I better go home because the children are going to get into trouble." Some of my family were on the Holland side and some were on the German side. One of my sisters was married to a Jewish fellow who was killed by the Nazis, and my older sister in my hometown was one of the Heil Hitlers, a Hitler supporter.

See what I mean, how terrible war is—to put sisters against one another? So Mommy went back to Germany, and a little later I had to put her in a nursing home over there. She writes, "Katie, if I could swim, I would swim back to America." She passed away six or eight years later.

And after the war, World War II, every week we sent packages to our relatives in Holland and Germany. You know, I knew what hunger was before. Every week for two years we sent packages. And not only one package—sometimes on Saturdays we had eight or ten packages. You can see where our money went. We sent sausage, smoked bacon—a butcher we knew smoked it for us—coffee, tea, all kinds of flour, sugar. Just so they could have something to eat. And shoes, bicycle tire tubes, things like that.

When I went back to my little hometown after the war, I ran into a schoolmate. She said, "Oh, Katie, I saw your sister going every week to the post office to pick up a package." My sister had said to her, "Oh yes, my rich American relatives sent the packages." That was their idea of us. But when she and her husband came later to visit us, they found out that the rich Americans didn't find the money in the street. We worked for every penny we earned. We worked for it, and we didn't mind.

Oh, we saved a few pennies and put them in the bank. And what did the banks do? They closed up—you know, during the depression. An hour before our bank closed, we managed to get out our Christmas savings. That was all. We lost the rest.

You can get anything you want in this country if you work for it—at least that's the way it used to be. But at the time of the depression there was no unemployment insurance, no social security benefits. Those of us who were immigrants often had no parents, no brothers and sisters, not even a family started in this country. We had no one to depend on except ourselves and those friends of other nationalities who were in the same boat.

And you'd be surprised in times like that how close-knit those friends got to be—almost as close-knit as brothers and sisters. We all had the same troubles. We found help and understanding in at least being able to discuss those troubles with somebody. And if the need got too bad in one place, well, you did what you could to help out. You brought them a basket of groceries, paid the rent for a month, or found a doctor who was willing to give his services, the payment to come later.

But in the last ten years those friends who gave assistance and pleasure have all died. You find when you get older that it's hard to replace friends, no matter how nice you are or how friendly you try to be. First of all, you can't make friends very well with younger people because of what the newspapers call the generation gap. And the older people don't want to strike up new acquaintances because, whether they admit it or not, they think, "In a few years it will be my turn to disappear, so why change now?" And they crawl into a hole; they sit by themselves and talk and think of the past.

We told you about sending packages to Germany and Holland after the war. Well, during the war—that was World War II—we got a letter from the Red Cross. The letter asked whether, if something happened to my sister living in Holland, we would assume responsibility for bringing up her children after the war. George wrote back that certainly we would do that. We didn't know what was going on. My sister's husband had had a tailor's shop in Holland. When Germany invaded Holland, he was killed. My sister had one little girl about three years old and was expecting another baby. We found out after the war that after they killed her husband, my sister was determined to fight the Nazis and had joined the Resistance.

The Resistance movement had established a loose underground network to smuggle out Jews, escaped prisoners of war, and Allied pilots who'd been shot down. They took these people to the North Sea beaches, where they were picked up by Allied ships. My sister, who was living in Amsterdam, helped to hide these people trying to escape from the country. It was very dangerous. The Nazis made searches of blocks of houses. If they had found anyone hiding in her house, my sister would have been immediately arrested and, within a day or two, shot. When we visited her after the war, she showed us a record player in the attic. It had a large cabinet, and the insides had been taken out. If it was necessary, that's where she hid the people she was helping to escape.

After the war was over, the Holland government selected six people to be honored—people who had joined the Resistance but were not Dutch citizens at the time. My sister was one of the six. She was made a Holland citizen by official proclamation, received a lifetime pension, free education for her children and free hospitalization, and was excluded from taxation for the rest of her life.

George and I went back to Europe for a visit in 1962. After about three months of traveling around, we had stopped in Hamburg, Germany. We were standing by the Elbe River on a command deck where, as a ship passes, they raise the flag and play the national anthem of that ship's country. While we were standing there, an American ship passed through, and we were singing the American national anthem. And George stood there, big tears rolling down his cheeks. "Let's go home, Katie," he says. "We don't belong here anymore."

5

Life in Little Italy: A Shoe Shine Boy Survives

ANTHONY SORRENTINO *was six years old when his family left Sicily to come to America in 1919. He grew up in a tough neighborhood, Chicago's Near West Side. The area had been "home" at one time or another for immigrant families from Ireland, Germany, France, and Britain. By 1920 it was occupied mostly by Italian immigrant families.*

A poor neighborhood, it had always had high rates of juvenile delinquency and crime. But when Prohibition made the manufacture and sale of liquor illegal in the 1920s, the Near West Side became so well known for bootlegging and violence that newspapers dubbed the area "the Bloody Twentieth Ward."

Although his childhood was at times very difficult—at age eleven Anthony helped to support his family as a shoe shine boy—curiosity and determination helped him to find his way. While working full-time he managed to finish high school and college and went on to take graduate courses at the University of Chicago.

Anthony's wife, Ann, was born in the United States, but her parents came from Sicily. The Sorrentinos were married in

1939; they have three children and three grandchildren. Both Anthony and Ann are very actively involved in the work of Italian-American organizations: the Joint Civic Committee of Italian-Americans and the Italo-American National Union.

Anthony has written numerous articles and several books on juvenile delinquency and crime. Ann Sorrentino is also an author: She is now putting together a cookbook featuring dishes from all the provinces of Italy. The recipes were collected from Italian-American women.

Currently Anthony is the executive director of the Commission on Delinquency Prevention for the State of Illinois and teaches three courses on delinquency at DePaul University in Chicago. Growing up in a tough neighborhood, a disadvantage in his youth, has been an asset to him during the forty-some years he has worked in the field of juvenile delinquency prevention.

His work has not gone unnoticed. He has been honored by the Italian government, which gave him the Star of Solidarity, and by his friends in the Italian community and in his professional field, who sponsored a testimonial banquet for him in 1963. Some 750 persons attended—that speaks well for a shoe shine boy from the Bloody Twentieth.

I was born on October 23, 1913, in the city of Marsala on the island of Sicily, just off the southern coast of Italy. Marsala is known throughout the world for its wine—a wine both sweet and dry. We lived right on the Mediterranean Sea, and my father and his brothers were engaged in the business of transporting this wine in small boats from the shore to the large ships out on the Mediterranean. Marsala at that time had no harbor.

My mother would often proudly tell me as I was growing up that when I was born, on one of my father's small boats the Italian flag was raised as a signal to my father, who was out to sea, that a son had been born. The birth of a boy was always celebrated in Italy with greater joy and clamor than the birth of a girl. My mother took the raising of the flag as an omen that I would one day grow up to be someone of importance.

My memories of Marsala are kind of faint, blurred; but one scene that I do recall is of goats. The goat man came every morning with a herd of goats, and the families would gather around with a bottle to have the milk squeezed from the goats right into the bottle. That's right, right from the goat—fresh. And so we children had, I remember, this goat milk.

Being on the Mediterranean, fresh fish was also always available, as were fresh vegetables, and, of course, pasta and so on. So I can't say that my life was like that of so many immigrants who came from Italy, especially those from the rural sections, those who knew such poverty and deprivation. Living in the city, and my father being sort of in business, we always had available adequate food. The homes were small, made of brick or masonry, but nicely furnished.

My father went to America alone and worked in Detroit for a short time. He decided to bring the family to America—as did, I'm sure, millions of other immigrants—to improve our social and economic position.

I was only six years old, but I remember taking the train—our first big train ride, you know—from Marsala to Palermo, or Naples I think it was. We stayed overnight one night in a hotel and then boarded the ship *Re d'Italia*, "the King of Italy." We came as a family: my father; mother; an older sister, Nancy; a younger brother, James; and myself.

The voyage on the ship was a long one, about three weeks, and we were probably in what was known as steerage—you know, the lower deck—where women and children slept together in one big section and the men in another. I have some faint memories of hundreds and thousands of people on this big ship. I remember being sick and sleepy and waiting, day by day.

I recall, too, the glee with which the announcement that we had passed through the Strait of Gibraltar was met; that was an important point in the journey. I believe there was a stop at Gibraltar, and it was at this point that we were introduced to bananas. Now, we may have had some bananas in Italy, but they were few and far between—very scarce. But for some reason bananas came aboard, and my brother, two years old at the time, was introduced to them. He took a great liking to them—so much so that when we came to Chicago, he would eat bananas by the bunch. It got to be that some of his friends nicknamed him Bananas, Jim Bananas.

We stayed with my Uncle Pietro in Brooklyn for about a week, and he wanted us to stay there; but my father had promised his other brother, Carlo, that we were coming to Chicago. So we came on to Chicago, and we lived for a few months with our aunt and uncle, who had no children and lived on the Near West Side of Chicago a few blocks from Hull House, the famous early settlement house that was founded in 1889 by Jane Addams.

We arrived in Chicago on a cold day; the climate was in sharp contrast to the warmer climate of Italy. And I remember all the noises: the trucks, and even in those days, the horse-drawn vehicles, you know, galloping through the streets, and the fire engines, and so on. I was suddenly hurled from a tranquil, quiet Marsala to a noisy, turbulent, urban Chicago. I'm sure that all registered in my child's mind. I was aware, certainly, that I had entered an alien new world.

Although you might live in an Italian neighborhood, the other children still regarded you as a greenhorn, a foreigner, when you first came to this country. You had the feeling that the kids in the streets and at school looked down on you. I remember the feelings of inferiority I had at first in school, feelings of being different, of not speaking the language. So in those early months I had to make quite an adjustment to overcome those feelings of not being accepted.

Although we came to live with relatives, there were still periods of uncertainty and loneliness at first for my family. I know my mother—she was thirty-seven at the time—had left all of her friends and relatives back in Italy, and she was shaken by the drabness of the streets, the physical environment of the city. And she would look out the window, you know, and call out for *Marsala bella*, "beautiful Marsala," where she could look out the window and see the beautiful Mediterranean Sea, the ships going to and fro—a more familiar life.

The thought was ever present in the minds of our family, and I'm sure in the minds of a lot of other immigrants as well, that we had come here temporarily. In fact, when we left Italy, my family didn't sell any of their furniture or their personal belongings. And my mother often referred to the beautiful furniture and possessions that she had left in Italy—handmade furniture—and we had to go out here and buy all new furniture of inferior machine-made quality.

I remember joking with my mother about going back to Italy after our family had been here for many decades, and by then she abhorred the thought, you see, of ever going back. She had made the adjustment. She died at the age of seventy-six, an American citizen. But she lived her entire life in the Italian community, the Near West Side, and a little later, further west. She learned only a few words of English. She never did go back to Italy, not even for a visit.

Upon arriving in Chicago, the first priority of my parents was to find employment, to have a regular income. Since no occupation similar to what my father did in Italy existed in Chicago, he did what most immigrants who came to the big cities did—he drifted into factory work. My father got a job in the candy factory where my uncle worked. My mother went to work in the Loop in a garment factory where my aunt worked.

Soon we moved into our own apartment. It was a three-bedroom, cold-water flat, you know. No central heating. We had to heat water in a pan on the stove.

When we weren't in school, we children were left at home alone while our parents worked. And in the beginning we were told to stay indoors, to beware of strangers, and not to open the door to persons unknown to us. One day there was a knock on the door, and all three of us—my sister, my brother, and I—listened in fear as a man's voice said: "Open the door—gas man." Well, we didn't know what he was talking about. We didn't dare open the door. We were fearful of strangers, as our parents had taught us to be. But finally our landlady came to the door and assured us in a kindly Italian tone of voice that it was all right to open the door.

So there was a strangeness, a fear of our new surroundings, a sense of being lost and alienated; and those feelings lasted for weeks and months, until we got acquainted and began to see the many pleasures and benefits, and the abundance, of life in America.

My parents learned quickly, as did other immigrants, that if you didn't have all the cash on hand, no matter, you could go to the department store on Halsted and Roosevelt Road and buy on credit. We bought furniture item by item on time, five dollars a month. I remember one of our interesting big purchases was the Victor Victrola; it cost seventy-five dollars. That was in 1921 or 1922. And it became our sole means of entertainment. We had no radio, no telephone, and of course, no television. The whole family would gather around, and we'd listen to records of Sicilian humor and folk tales, Italian song and opera, and Caruso, the famous Italian singer. So life was not affluent; it was not lavish—but still we had some pleasant moments.

My father often spoke of the importance of honesty and maintaining a good name. His guiding principles for the family were obedience, loyalty, love, respect, and honorable actions at all times. I recall one lesson he taught me about respect. When entering the home, we children were expected to greet our father and all other elders with the saying *Vossia mi benedica,* "Give me your blessing." But after a few years in America I began to think that this was old-fashioned, and one day I refused to say it. My father ordered me out of the house and told me to come back only when I was prepared to enter like a Christian. I waited outside, somewhat rebellious. I tried to enter again without saying those words and was sent out again. Finally, after freezing on the back porch for a while, I entered and dutifully said, *"Vossia mi benedica."*

My father responded, *"Dio ti benedice,"* "God will bless you."

I can recall the sights and sounds of the city streets in our neighborhood during those early years. There was the junk peddler with his chant, "Rags a line." He was looking for discarded rags and old iron to purchase, rags and iron, but he said the words so fast that it sounded to us like "rags a line." I remember, too, the funeral procession that was led down the street by an orchestra playing funeral chants and somber music that created an eerie, sorrowful feeling throughout the neighborhood. Then there was Bruno the hot dog man, who sold his hot dogs with the chant *Chi mangia muore mai,* "He who eats never dies." For five cents you could get a delicious hot dog with all the fixings, including Italian pepper. There was also the waffle man, who came in a gaily colored wagon—when he opened the window, a shelf magically dropped down. A very delicious waffle with powdered sugar cost only a penny or two.

In the summertime, life on the Near West Side took place in the streets and in front of one's doorstep. To escape the heat of their apartments on warm summer evenings, people sat on their doorsteps, exchanging conversation with their neighbors and people passing by on the sidewalks. Part of the scene, too, would be the vendor with his pushcart, selling an assortment of Italian beans: *lupini,* a giant Italian bean soaked in salt water; *ceci,* chick-peas; and pumpkin seeds. His cry was *passatempo,* "pass time," or buy something to pass your time. The people would buy a bagful of beans to munch on as they sat on their doorsteps, and soon someone would come along with a little homemade wine. The kids would saunter down the block to buy lemonade. In front of every grocery store there was a lemonade stand, where you might buy lemonade, watermelon, boiled corn, taffy apples, penny candy—things like that.

And in the fall of the year, the grape peddlers would come around selling grapes by the box. People would buy 50 boxes, 100 boxes, 200 boxes to make homemade wine. We kids would follow these trucks, and when a purchase was made, we would help unload the boxes. We were rewarded with all the grapes we could eat, and perhaps some to take home. We'd carry the boxes into somebody's basement and line them up. This is where the families would make their wine. Homemade wine was quite a common thing in those days.

Well, those are some of the scenes and recollections of a boy growing up in the 1920s on the Near West Side. But there was another side to our neighborhood, too: violence. Those ten or twelve years of Prohibition in the 1920s, when federal regulations forbade the manufacture and sale of alcohol, begot violence.

Alcohol was manufactured secretly, illegally, in my neighborhood—and in many neighborhoods. People had stills—distilleries for making alcohol or whiskey—in their basements or even in ordinary flats. I remember sometimes, going home from school, you would pass certain houses and smell yeast fermenting—it was used to make the alcohol. Occasionally you might find alcohol running along the gutter; that meant the police had raided somebody's still, had knocked it over to destroy it.

We had been living in America for about five years when my father had a stroke. It was 1924. He had a stroke and stayed at home in bed for six months before he died. I realized after my father's stroke that things were going to be tough for the family. I had heard about boys in my neighborhood who would shine shoes. So I decided to embark on the career of becoming a shoe shine boy. But my father wouldn't listen to it. He protested and called it a lowly occupation. He used a word—I don't know how to translate it into English—but it meant a boy of the streets, you know, one who takes up a lowly, almost immoral trade. So he put thumbs down on that.

But I kept watching the other boys, and I saw that they were making money. I could see that my father was beginning to weaken to the idea. He couldn't work, and our family had no income. So I sold lemonade, as kids do—penny lemonade, you know—to make the $1.10 that I needed to buy the brushes and the polishes and the cloths. I told my father, "If it bothers you that I will be walking the streets with this box over my shoulder, I'll carry it out in a paper bag so that no one will identify me with such a lowly trade, and I'll go out of the neighborhood where I won't be known."

Well, I began on a weekend, and I made a couple of dollars on Saturday. I started on Madison and Halsted, but I realized that a lot of other kids were shining shoes in that area. It was competitive. So I ambled over to the Randolph Street Market, which in those days was the major supplier of fruits and vegetables for the city's restaurants and grocery stores. Farmers came in with their horses and wagons to sell to the Greek, Jewish, and Italian men who owned the stores. I figured that it might be a good place for a shoe shine boy because these men would have dirty shoes at the end of the day. I made probably three dollars a weekend, Saturdays and Sundays, shining shoes at the market.

And shortly thereafter, I was walking past a shoe shine

parlor and hat-cleaning establishment when the Greek pro-
prietor called me aside and asked me if I was interested in a
job. Now, this was a promotion. He asked me to demonstrate
how I could shine shoes, and I put forth my best skills, you
know, and I got the job. I made about five or six dollars a
weekend, almost double what I had made before, and that
was considered pretty good money in 1924 and 1925.

After my father died, this money from the shoe-shining
establishment really helped the family. I should mention,
too, that during this time I used to go junking. It was a
common practice among the kids in the neighborhood to
wander up and down the alleys—you'd walk for miles and
miles—looking for lead pipes, metal, rags, and bottles to sell.

My sister was thirteen, and I was about eleven, when the
hard times set in. My sister dropped out of school and got a
job in a factory, a paper box factory. My mother, who was
never too aggressive, during this period became more dependent; so my sister and I became the real breadwinners of the
family. We supported the family on about twenty dollars a
week at the time.

I forgot to mention that when my father had his stroke, an
uncle of mine, Albert, lived with us. He came here to work
and to make money to send back to his family in Marsala. But
at the time my father died, Uncle Albert was due to go back,
and he returned to Marsala. The aunt and uncle we came to
live with when we first arrived in this country had also
returned to Marsala. And so we were left completely alone in
America with no relatives whatsoever. But you would find in
an Italian community, at least in those days, a feeling of
kinship among the people that came from the same town or
province. And in times of need they helped one another. We

received some help from the people of Marsala, our country-men, *paesani.*

But anyway, in the year 1928 I dropped out of school. It was supposed to be a period of prosperity, but there was no prosperity in our particular family, and so I felt the need to find a job. But here I was, fifteen, and it was futile. I kept pounding on the same doors; I thought persistence might pay off. I might never have gotten a job if I hadn't met a man who had a very, very beneficial impact on me. His name was Henry A. Meyer. He was a theological student at a local Methodist church. Now, I—our family—was Catholic. We were identified as members of our local church, Our Lady of Pompeii Church, even if we didn't go there with complete regularity. I was baptized, made my Communion, and was confirmed as a Catholic; so we were a little distant as far as the other religions were concerned.

But I met this man, and he was friendly and warm and accepting, and I was just drawn to him—I suppose because of my need for a father figure. He took me downtown—an experience that was relatively new to me—to an employment agency that hired clerks and office personnel. I knew I wouldn't get a job if I told the truth about my age, and so I said I was sixteen. And lo and behold, I got a job as an office boy at an office downtown.

I'll never forget the great stock market crash of 1929, the Great Depression. People were jumping out of windows after losing their fortunes. But I was lucky. I had gotten this office job paying $12 a week, so I could give my mother $10 a week. I walked downtown every day dressed in a suit—walked to save the seven-cent carfare. And I'd go out to eat in a restaurant; that was a new experience, you know. I allowed myself twenty-five cents a day for lunch. Well, after six months I was raised to $14 a week, and six months later to $18 a week. I was making $18 as a regular weekly income during the depression, when some families had no income at all.

I had finished elementary school, so I began to go to high school in the evenings after work. I went to Crane Evening High School. I worked from nine to five, walked home to grab something to eat, walked to Crane, where I spent about two and a half hours, and then walked back home. I kept up that schedule four nights a week, Monday through Thursday, until I had enough credits to be admitted to a junior college—Herz Junior College, one of the city's early junior colleges.

It was at about this time, as I moved into the world downtown, that I began to feel acutely self-conscious about living in a poor neighborhood, an Italian neighborhood, and was disturbed by the contrast in the different social worlds that I moved in. We still lived in a relatively poor home, meagerly furnished, and then I would go downtown and sit at a desk and sometimes go to the homes of the big executives on Lake Shore Drive and in Oak Park. They lived in what then seemed to me to be mansions. And here I was with my dependent mother, no rich uncle or older brother, nobody else—just myself, a boy. How was I going to make it in this competitive world? How would I ever get to the point where I could have some of those nice things?

These experiences created a certain kind of dilemma that I was able to resolve, but not without a lot of soul-searching and not without some emotional problems. I found legitimate avenues for the achievement of my desires for a better life, but other immigrant boys who weren't so lucky often became frustrated and turned to crime.

Our neighborhood was a rough and tough neighborhood during Prohibition. The newspapers referred to it as the Bloody Twentieth Ward. And some of us young men growing up at that time felt that our own careers would be hampered or hindered by the bad reputation of the area. It was also at this time that I became aware of discrimination and stereotyping in my own life. So we organized a group called *Fratelli Guidante,* "Guiding Brothers," and we used to meet at Hull House in an attempt to overcome the stigma that the outside world had put on Italians—all Italians—living on the Near West Side of Chicago in those days. The group later evolved into a community organization that's still functioning, the Near West Side Community Committee.

In 1934, the same year that I graduated from high school, the company that I worked for went bankrupt, and I joined the army of the unemployed. I was disillusioned and depressed. But then I met two men who greatly influenced my life: Clifford R. Shaw and his assistant, Henry D. McKay. They were prominent research sociologists with the Institute for Juvenile Research and the Chicago Area Project. They were responsible for getting me started on my next job, which involved working with street gangs on the Near West Side, my own neighborhood.

For me, that was the beginning of a lifetime of community and youth work. I went on to college, and when I graduated, I became a sociologist with the Institute for Juvenile Research. I maintained my contacts in the Italian-American community, and I worked to promote the well-being of our people—as well as all ethnic and racial groups.

You know, earlier we were all led to believe—all immigrants coming here—that we were to forget, to live down our past heritage. We were here in America to become Americanized. This was the melting pot, and we were all going to melt into a new American mass. But now it's recognized that we're a pluralistic society, and America is, as John F. Kennedy said, a "nation of immigrants." So why not preserve the heritage and the culture of each of the great ethnic groups, because each has contributed—and that's what makes America great.

6

Morning Glories
at Minidoka

MIKI AKIYAMA UCHIDA *was born in 1903 in the village of Shimizumura, Japan. She came to this country as a young bride in 1921. Her husband, Tadatomo, the grandson of samurai (a class of aristocratic warriors in Japan), had come to America in the early 1900s as a student. He stayed on to build a thriving greenhouse business.*

Miki came to a country that did not welcome Orientals. In 1907 the United States had negotiated the so-called Gentlemen's Agreement with Japan, by which the Japanese government agreed not to issue passports to Japanese laborers to come to America. Japanese people already living in the United States, including the Uchidas, were prevented by federal laws from owning land or becoming American citizens.

Despite prejudice and discrimination, Miki Uchida lived and worked near Seattle, Washington, for twenty years— Tadatomo for thirty years. Their children had been born and were growing up in this country. The family considered America its home.

But when Japan attacked Pearl Harbor in 1941, the Uchidas' lives changed drastically. In the atmosphere of fear and hysteria that followed the attack, President Roosevelt signed

Executive Order 9066, which forced 110,000 Japanese-Americans, of whom about two-thirds were native-born, to move from their homes into internment camps.

The move was intended to protect this country from Japanese-Americans—and to protect Japanese-Americans from other Americans. The Uchidas and their four children were taken to Minidoka Relocation Center in Idaho, where they lived for three years.

Miki's second son served in the American armed forces during the war, as did 25,000 other Japanese-Americans. He was part of the famed 442nd Combat Team, a highly decorated Japanese-American unit, and was sent to Japan during the American occupation following the war.

Japanese-Americans proved their loyalty to America—a country that discriminated against them—in a way that no other nationality had ever been asked to do. Neither German-Americans nor Italian-Americans were sent to camps, although the United States was also at war with Germany and Italy. When in recognition of this loyalty the American government granted Japanese-Americans the right to U.S. citizenship, Miki and Tadatomo studied the Constitution and answered a judge's questions so that they, too, might become citizens.

Miki's husband died several years ago. She lives today in the basement apartment of a small, two-story home on Chicago's North Side. The three mailboxes in the hallway all read Uchida.

Miki is a gentle, religious person with much strength and inner peace. Although she grew up in Japan in a Buddhist family—her uncle was a Buddhist monk—Miki was converted to Christianity in 1947. She is a very active member of the Lakeside Japanese Christian Church in Chicago.

Miki is not bitter about the difficult years; she prefers to think of the good that came from her life at Minidoka. She has always loved flowers, and in the summer she plants a small garden in the backyard, just as she did during her internment at Minidoka.

In Japan when I was a child, we have a field of mulberry trees, you know, where you raise silkworms. And my father likes flowers very much; so in one spot in this mulberry field, he put all kinds of flowers. He had azaleas, sweet peas, peonies—all kinds of flowers, unusual kinds, even celery. People don't eat celery in Japan, not at that time. But he grew celery one year. When he brought it into the house, my mother says, "Take it away; it smells like medicine."

I was the only one in the family besides my father that liked flowers. And my father always called to me to show me that this one is blooming and that one is about to bloom. When he'd go to the store, walking along the way, every place where people have nice flowers, he'd stop and talk. He loved flowers. People would come from town to buy his flowers, and he'd sell them so cheap that my mother would get mad. But you know what he did with the money? He'd buy more seeds and flowerpots. He loved flowers. I think that's where I got it; I love flowers, too.

But there was something on that little farm that I didn't like. I used to have to go out into the rice fields to help. Not all the time, but just in the busy season, the planting season. I'd stay home from school and go help in the fields. The one thing that I hated was those leeches. You know the leech? They live in the rice fields. We wore coverings over our legs, but those leeches—they're pretty foxy. They'd get in under the coverings. They don't hurt; they feel more like an itch.

But they suck your blood. Once they attach themselves to you, they're hard to get off.

I tell you, those leeches are something. I used to dream about them. I hated those leeches so much that I said I wasn't going to marry a Japanese farmer—I didn't want to work in the rice fields with the leeches. And I think my wish came true when my husband came to Japan to look for a wife.

My husband, Tadatomo Uchida, was working in a greenhouse in the United States. He told a friend, who was also my mother's friend, that he was looking for a wife. He was asking about me. I was eighteen then, but my mother refused. She didn't ask me or anything; she just refused. She said, "No, America is too far away." But one day I was walking someplace with my mother and her friend, and her friend asked me would I like to go to America. And I told them, yes, that I would like to go. The chance came when my future husband himself came over from America, and the talk started all over again. Finally my mother decided, okay, and that's how I came to this country.

I already knew something about America. When I was a little girl six or seven years old, my older brother used to send me beautiful color postcards from America. They were such beautiful, beautiful pictures. I thought that America was a beautiful place, and I had admiration for it.

But my mother knew it took a pretty long time, a long distance, to come to this country; that's why she didn't want to let me go. And I was her youngest child, the last one left at home. My husband said we would come back in three years to visit them. But my mother said, "If you come back in five or ten years, that's pretty good."

She was right—I didn't go back to see her. I had four children right away, and you can't leave your children when they're young. And then my husband needed my help in the greenhouse. So I never made it to Japan, and they died. My mother and father died. And that was really sad. They both died in wartime, and I didn't even know it. The war was going on, you know, and we didn't hear anything from Japan—no letters, nothing. But that's what you expect when you come from far away.

I was married in January, and we came to this country in April. It was 1921. Of course, we came in a boat—no airplanes then. Fourteen days in a boat, and the first few days make you seasick. It was a Japanese boat, a new boat and a big one. But still, when we got out onto the ocean, it was rocking, and everything was sliding from one side of the boat to the other. You couldn't even eat food on the table because all the dishes would go down onto the floor. So they were making sandwiches and things that you could eat by hand. But at that time I can't even eat, so sick. It took four or five days to start to calm down. And then you don't feel so bad, and everybody got up and walked around, and it was nice.

On the boat there were many people, Japanese people, who had gone to Japan to visit and were returning to America. Some people had left children in Japan. I remember one woman was crying all the time. She didn't eat, just cried all the way. She had left her children. I never forget that, even now.

Those tourists on the boat—what do you call them, people already living in America?—they gave you all kinds of advice. "When you go to America," they say, "go work in somebody's home, do housework, and you will learn English. But don't work for skinny people; work for fat people. They're easier to get along with than skinny people."

When we came to the port of Seattle, Washington, it was nighttime, and we could see the lights of the city, beautiful lights over all the hills. It was so beautiful. But you know what? I was kind of sorry to leave the boat. I had a feeling of fear; I didn't know what will happen after I get onto American soil, you know. I had the feeling that I'd like to stay on the boat a little longer.

Then we have to go to the immigration office for an examination right away, and I was a little bit afraid. Of course, I didn't have any sickness; I was all right. Some people had to take medicine and stay in quarantine for a couple of weeks, but I passed all right.

A friend of my husband's came after us with a car, and we drove five miles to where my husband lived. It was April when I came, so all the cherry blossoms and pear trees and all the spring flowers were blooming. It was beautiful. They have lots of moisture in Washington. We were one mile from the Pacific Ocean. In springtime it's warm and moist. I remember when I first came, everybody have a beautiful lawn; in Japan you don't see that. I get homesick for Seattle in the springtime. You could raise all kinds of flowers. In Chicago you have to wait until May or June, but in Seattle you already start having those primroses, and everything start growing and blooming outside in February. I think Seattle is still more my home than Chicago.

My husband had a greenhouse business in Seattle. I don't know English, but my husband tells me, when a customer comes in, I have to say the flower's name in English. So I try to learn all the names of the flowers. Some of the names are hard to remember. We have a big poster in the greenhouse, and I write down in Japanese the name, and then the English sound, and that way I remember.

I came to this country during the busy season in the greenhouse, and I didn't have a chance to go to school to learn English right away. And then in June I was going to school, but I got pregnant. At that time I had to go downtown to go to school, and after I got pregnant I couldn't ride the streetcar because I'd get sick. So there goes my school. I had four children in almost five years. So I can't go to school, and that's why my English is poor. I can't spell. I'm afraid to spell because I make mistakes.

I learned to speak some English from a Caucasian family that lived next door. People from Norway, very nice couple. And when my children started going to school, I make them study the *ABC*s. And I study with them. One day I write down capital *A*, the next day is *B*. I make them write it down, and I do, too. I wanted to learn English so bad that I talked to my children in English. I tried to use only English, you know. I learned to speak and read English with my children up to the third grade—I couldn't go any further.

When my second son memorized speeches, I have to learn myself or else I can't help him. I remember Lincoln's Gettysburg Address. Those *l*s never go out of my head. The Japanese language doesn't have the *l* sound, so I had a pretty hard time.

I learned English from the funny paper, too. I'd look at the pictures off and on, and, you know, pretty soon I could understand what they were saying—and that's how I started to read.

When Japan attacked Pearl Harbor in 1942 and war broke out between Japan and the United States, we had a farm near Seattle, Washington. We were getting ready to take some vegetables to the public market in Seattle when we heard the news. We didn't know what to do. But everything was so quiet, we just went to the market. And you know, nobody made a fuss. When people wanted to buy something, they did; and they didn't say anything. I thought the American people were very big about it. But of course, they knew it wasn't our fault—it was the people in Japan, army people, doing it. Once a drunk said something to us, but most people didn't.

I didn't know what to expect after the attack. I was afraid. Some Japanese people said maybe we'd be chased into the Puget Sound or the ocean—that we'd all be killed. Rumors were going around, you know.

When evacuation time came, we couldn't take anything but a suitcase that we could carry. They took all the leaders of the Japanese community first. Some even that day—the people who taught fencing, judo, or Japanese dancing, and so forth. We got everything ready for my husband, but he wasn't taken away with the first ones. We were so happy.

They told us to take our radios, guns, knives so many inches long, things like that, to a certain place. And they wanted to see our books. We couldn't have certain kinds of books, but we didn't know what kind. So you know what we did? My husband dug a big hole, and we buried all our books in the Japanese language. We just dug a big hole, threw the books in, and covered them up with dirt. It's hard to burn books, you know; so we buried them. Some of those books we can't get anymore.

They'd tell you on such and such a day you have to be ready to go. You can't take any more than you can carry—the rest you have to leave behind. Everyone had to have his or her own enamelware plate and cup. So we got those. And they took us by bus to the assembly center at the fairground in Puyallup, outside Seattle. The first thing they did was to give you straw to make a mattress. Then each person got an army cot. You put the straw mattress on it, and that's where you slept. We stayed in a small barrack, a small building—six of us. The floor had cracks with weeds growing up through them. I tell you, it made you feel really low.

But worse than that was going to the mess hall to eat. Everybody had to go at one time, and some people were standing outside in the sun for half an hour. Some of the people who weren't strong—they fainted. And all you got to eat was maybe some boiled cabbage and a couple of canned wieners. You'd have to wait in those lines, eat poor food, wash your plate and cup, and go back to the barrack. It was a little too much. We were there, I don't remember exactly, but more than a month. The permanent camp was a much better place. I heard a rumor afterward that somebody that worked for this assembly center made money by not feeding us properly.

My second son was working on a railroad in Montana when we heard that we were going to be moved to a permanent camp, and so I wrote to him to come back. I was afraid we'd be separated. I didn't know where we were going, and I was afraid he might be sent to another camp. So I told him to come to his family, and he came.

Maybe you should hear about that one, my second son. This boy was in Lincoln High School in Seattle, Washington, and he was an honor student. He wanted to go into electrical engineering. He had applied to a special college where a job was guaranteed to the graduates. But one day the principal of Lincoln High School called him into his office. And do you know what he told him? "Japan and America aren't on such good terms now, and after you graduate from that college, they aren't going to be able to find a job for you; so why don't you go into sheet metal work?" This was before Pearl Harbor. My son got so mad that he said he wasn't going to go to the high school graduation. I gave him money to buy a suit for graduation, but he said he was going to buy work clothes instead and go to work for the railroad. And that's what he did. He said he was born in the United States, grew up here, went to school here, and he had never felt he was Japanese—until then.

He makes a good living now; he owns a garage and service station. He was so good with mechanical things that he taught himself how to repair automobiles. His children are all going to college. And he says one good thing about it: When his children complain about school, he puts them to work at the service station. He tells them if they don't want to do that kind of work, then they'd better finish college.

So my son came back, and we all went together to the permanent camp—Minidoka Relocation Center in Idaho—my husband and I and our four children. At that time my oldest son was nineteen, my second son was eighteen, my daughter was seventeen, and my youngest son was sixteen. My children volunteered to help build the camp, and so we were the first batch to go to Minidoka. Our building was ready, but the others weren't, and they were working day and night to finish the camp to let the other people come in.

I tell you something. When we first got there, it was really sad. We went on a train. We don't know where we are going. They come and close the shades down. I don't know how many hours we ride, but then the train stopped. We saw no building, no trees, nothing; but that's where the train stopped, and that's where we got off. It was in the middle of the desert. Everybody got off, and army trucks, open army trucks, were waiting there to pick us up. We were driving along through the desert with a yellow car behind us and the sand flying. We got to the camp, and just one barrack was ready. Hundreds of people working, and bulldozers. We go right away to the washroom, but the showers weren't ready yet, you know; so everybody was trying to wash themselves in the laundry tubs. Sand was everywhere. The food wasn't bad at all—it was okay. But at that time you didn't feel like eating very much anyway.

At each corner of our barrack stood a soldier with a gun. The gun had a bayonet on it. Full guard day and night. Barbed wire fences all round the camp. And when nighttime came, the coyotes howling like a baby crying and the soldiers with bayonets. You know, I really feel—what do you call—despair. I feel low, a sad feeling.

We lived at Minidoka three years. We lived in a barrack. Each barrack, one long building, was divided up into units for six families. Each family had one big room. Our family—all six of us—slept on army cots in one room. The units were divided by pressed wood, sheets of pressed wood. That's all there was between you and your neighbors. You could hear everything the people next door were saying. Each room had one of those old-fashioned wood stoves for heat. And you know, when we first got there, they had had a sandstorm.

Sand blowing and flying all over and coming into the house. I have to sweep out all the sand to make our unit ready to live in. At the beginning you feel kind of lost and sad, a really sad feeling.

But you know what we start to do? Everybody work in the field to make irrigation ditches, you know, and to sow seeds in the ground to raise vegetables. When it rains, it's so muddy in front of the buildings that you can't even walk; but some people bring sagebrush, cut them up, and put them on top of the ground for people to walk on. And the next year we plant some flowers, morning glories and things—yes, we did it. And I even made like a cement pond for fish, but they died on me. We never just sit still, you know; we work to make it better. Yes. My husband, he likes to do carpentry work, and so he made us some furniture—a dresser, a chair, things like that. He made some nice things.

We all worked at the camp. My husband had a friend in the mess hall, and he wanted to be with him; so he helped with the cooking, and I was working as a waitress. They gave us sixteen dollars a month for working in the mess hall. Office people got paid a little bit more, and teachers earned nineteen dollars a month. They gave us army clothes, khaki things, and three dollars a month for clothing.

At that time I didn't think this way, but now I look at the three years in camp as a good thing for Japanese people, in a way. They were always working so hard, working to make money to send their children to school, never having any fun. All they do is work. They were a very tired people, you know. And those three years in the camp were just like a vacation, really. I don't know what other people think, but I think so. We didn't have much work to do, and everything we needed was provided.

They had classes. I was knitting so many sweaters, ski sweaters for my children, and even a suit for myself. And a lady was teaching a class on traditional Japanese doll-making, and I made dolls. The children had movies, activities in the recreation room, and softball teams. The old men had a softball team, too. They all playing something. They had a school for the children. They pulled the children out of their regular school, you know, to take them to the camp. My daughter graduated high school from the camp school.

I don't really know what kind of an impact it had on my children. But maybe they got to know a little more about Japanese people and Japanese culture. We had been living in the country near Seattle, and there weren't many Japanese people in one spot. But in the camp—all Japanese people; everyone doing things together. I think maybe it gave them more of a feeling for Japanese things.

This war was hard on us, but the American government found out Japanese people were loyal, that Japanese people living here and born here think of United States as their home. Japanese boys went to war for this country and did a good job. So after the war the American government give us a chance to get our citizenship papers. When my husband and I came to this country, we weren't allowed to become citizens or to own land. When my husband first came, he was a student and came with a student's passport. But later he decided to stay and work. We weren't expecting to stay for all our lives. We were like other Japanese people who came to this country to work, make money, and go back to Japan.

You know, when you can't have citizenship or own land, you feel temporary-like. But after your children are born here and growing up, you get accustomed to this country. So, many Japanese people, even if they go back to Japan, they can't stand it, and sometimes they come back to the United States.

And then, you know, before the war, Japanese-American people graduate from university—do good in school—but nobody would hire them for good jobs; they'd hire Caucasians. Japanese people, even the ones born in this country, with good education, were doing lower-class work. At that time, before the war, we thought we were really discriminated against, never to get a nice job. But after the war Japanese-American boys and girls going to college could get jobs as nice as Caucasians got.

I think we got those chances because of the Japanese-American boys that fought in the 442nd regiment during the war. My son, second son, the one that didn't go to his graduation, was in the 442nd. You see, I have two boys eligible to go to war at that time. My first son volunteered to go to the army, and so my second son came and told me that he didn't volunteer because he knew I didn't want both my sons to go. I didn't have to say anything. They know how I feel about it, I suppose. And I was thankful. But my first son, the one who volunteered, we found out he had bad eyesight, and the army wouldn't take him. And in the meantime, my second son was drafted.

You know, at that time our children were all citizens; they were American-born. But the government put them in camp the same as mother and father. And then, once the children were in camp, they were asked were they loyal to this country, would they go to war for this country? Many

Japanese people were against their sons' fighting in the war because of the way the American government had treated us, even American-born Japanese. But my sons felt that Japan didn't want American-born Japanese as Japanese citizens. And if the United States didn't want them as citizens, then they would have no country. They felt the United States was their country, and so they wanted to volunteer to fight for it.

My second son became a sergeant right away, but he didn't go overseas. He stayed in this country to train the new recruits. But during the American occupation of Japan, he was sent first to a language school, and then on to Japan. He was in Japan for almost two years; he was a warrant officer over there. He said, "Mother, I'm so glad you were in America, not Japan, during the war."

After the war, you know, they wanted everybody to move from the camp. My son, the first son, came to Chicago and got a job. He said to come here because we would have a place to stay, and we did. I got a job as a dressmaker, and my husband went to work as a cabinetmaker. And we've stayed here ever since. When we could, we took out our citizenship papers, my husband and I both.

My brother, he went back to Japan. He came to this country in 1907, when I was four years old. My grandfather had lost everything, and when my brother grew up, he decided to come to this country to—how do you say—build up a house again, regain the family fortune. He worked for other people at first, but then he leased 500 acres in Imperial Valley, California, and raised melons. He was doing that until the Second World War broke out, and he had to go into a camp, like us. He lost everything. He had sent all his money to a bank in Japan; he was going to live in Japan after he retired on the interest from that money. But after the war, the money—Japanese money—wasn't worth much. I felt so sorry for my brother because he worked so hard for so many years and then lost everything. On top of that, he was working on a strawberry farm after the war and had a stroke. He went back to Japan later. I visited him there. He lived to be ninety. But he said he wished he had stayed in this country; it would have been better. I felt so sorry to leave him.

But I'm thankful to be living in the United States. The country is wonderful to us. All my children grow up here and have nice homes and families. When my husband and I went back to Japan nine years ago, I thought, "It's all right to visit, but not to live over there. I won't go back to live." In the little Japanese villages—how do you say—even if you sleep late, they talk about it.

7

From <u>But and Ben</u> to Bungalow

In 1929 LACHLAN McARTHUR, *his mother, his three sisters, and his brother left Blantyre, Scotland, to come to the United States. They arrived just in time to greet the depression. But the hard times did not diminish the joy they felt on their arrival; the family had come to America to be reunited with Lachlan's father, who had left Blantyre six years earlier to work in the coal mines of southern Illinois.*

Lachlan was a freshman in high school when his family left Scotland, and he resumed his education when the family settled in Benton, Illinois. Lachlan's experience in American schools was not a totally pleasant introduction to life in the United States. He never received an American high school diploma, and he believes that the basic education he had in Scotland was superior to any he received, or might have received, in this country.

Lachlan has worked in this country as a laborer in the steel mills and in several factories, but for the past thirty years he has been a water pump salesman. He met his wife, Rebecca Grieve McArthur, at a Scottish dance. They were married in 1941.

"When we were going together, we did an awful lot of

Scottish dancing," Rebecca remembers. "It seemed like almost every Saturday night there was a Scotch dance or card game." They still attend Scottish affairs, although fewer Scottish dances have been held in recent years.

The McArthurs have two children—a son and a daughter—and one grandchild. Their granddaughter, Heather, named for the wild flower that grows in Scotland, is taking Scottish Highland dancing lessons and sometimes goes with her grandparents to Scottish dances. Lachlan and Rebecca consider it important for their granddaughter to know something of her Scottish heritage and to have pride in it, although she is only half Scottish.

Lachlan's memories of Scotland are mixed—some pleasant, some not so pleasant—but they are all vivid.

I was born November 16, 1915, in Blantyre, Scotland. Blantyre's claim to fame is that it's the birthplace of David Livingstone, the African missionary and explorer. It's a small coal-mining village about eight miles southwest of the big city of Glasgow.

My first name, Lachlan, is about as Scottish as you can get. It's a family name. In Scotland, it's kind of a tradition that the firstborn son is named after the father's father. My grandfather's name was Lachlan McArthur; so when I was born, the firstborn son, my parents named me Lachlan McArthur. But my father had nine brothers, and they all got married, and they all had firstborn sons—who were all named Lachlan McArthur.

Counting my uncle and my grandfather, I know of eleven Lachlan McArthurs in our family besides myself. And with that many Lachlan McArthurs, none of us have middle names or initials. But we didn't all come to this country; only two others came besides my Uncle Lachlan and me.

I have some very pleasant memories of my life in Blantyre. But when I think of the quarters that we lived in—those are dreary memories. We lived in a tenement, and the apartment that we occupied was what they call a *but and ben* in Scotland. It consisted of one big room, a combination kitchen, living room, and bedroom, with beds recessed into the wall; a parlor; and a scullery, which was like a utility room. The parlor was kept only for company; we children rarely got to go into the parlor. Although there was a regular wash house where the women washed the clothing, we also had a big boiler in our scullery that you could put a fire under to boil clothing. The scullery was where we stored coal for the fireplace. We had no electricity; cooking and lighting were done with gas. And what heating we had came from an open fireplace.

My father was a coal miner. He had always heard about the United States being a land of opportunity, and he had a couple of brothers who had come to work in the coal mines in southern Illinois. They wrote and told him how much money they were making; so in 1923 he packed up and came to make some of it himself. The rest of the family stayed behind in Scotland. My father worked in the coal mines in Franklin County, around Benton, Illinois.

Many Scottish people came from the coal-mining areas of Scotland to work in America's coal mines. If you go to the coal-mining areas of Pennsylvania and southern Illinois, you'll find all kinds of people that have come over here from Scotland.

The working conditions in the coal mines in America were

far superior to the working conditions in Scotland, according to my father. The coal veins in Scotland were very shallow; there might be only three feet of coal. That meant the men had to do a lot of the work with picks and shovels, on their knees or lying on their backs. In this country the coal veins were quite a bit larger; machinery was used more often to cut the coal, and automatic loaders to load it. I don't know the pay scale in actual dollars and cents, but my father's hourly wage was probably half again as much in this country as what he made in Scotland.

While he worked in southern Illinois, my father sent money home for us to subsist on, and some of it we saved. If things went his way, he intended to have the whole family join him. But his mother, who was still in Scotland, took seriously ill in 1927. So he came back to Scotland and stayed until she passed away. He returned to this country in 1928, and we followed the next year. My mother sailed with us five children in November of 1929. I had three sisters: one was eighteen, one was sixteen, and one was twelve. I was fourteen, and my younger brother was ten.

I didn't have any choice about coming to America. In those days parents didn't consult their children. You went where they had to go. It was a bad experience for children the age that we were to be picked up in Scotland and put down in a little town in southern Illinois and picked up again the next year to go to Chicago. I had a few bad years.

But all that was after the actual trip—I had fun on the voyage over here. We left from Glasgow aboard the *Caledonia* and landed in New York City. It was the first time that I had ever been on an oceangoing ship, although I'd been on smaller steamers, which are quite common in Scotland. We had some rough weather. I think the whole family had a little seasickness on the second day. Mine didn't last but a couple of hours. Most of my time was spent in running around the deck and exploring the ship. I enjoyed the food and the whole experience. I think the trip took seven days.

After we had gone through customs and immigration on Ellis Island, we were met by an aunt who lived in Philadelphia. She took us by train to her home, where we spent a couple of days before we came on through to Illinois.

Traveling across the country on the train, seeing the tall corn, which we didn't have in Scotland, was quite an experience. Somebody had to tell us it was corn, you know. The farming in this country looked a lot different than farming in Scotland. We had small farms in Scotland. The fields were laid out with boundaries of hedges and rows of stones so that you could tell which field belonged to which farmer. But you couldn't in this country. Everything was new and different. Even the cattle, the pigs, and the sheep all looked different than they did in Scotland. Yeah, getting on that train in Philadelphia and going to southern Illinois was quite an experience, quite a change.

Rebecca, my wife, tells about her family coming across country on the train. She says her mother looked out at all the wooden houses and exclaimed, "Oh, I hope I won't have to live in a wooden house." We didn't have wooden houses in Scotland in those days—most of the houses were made of stone. But she did have to live in a wooden house. In fact, Rebecca says that she thinks every house in this country that they ever lived in was made of wood.

The home my father had rented for our family was a really nice bungalow—a palace compared to what we had left in Scotland. It was a three-bedroom bungalow with a basement, electricity, forced-air heat—the whole works.

It was a happy reunion when we reached southern Illinois. My father had been over here working since 1923. So, except during my father's visits, my mother had been without a husband, and we children without a father, for six years. We arrived in 1929, the year the stock market crashed and the Great Depression really hit. But we survived the depression in good shape.

My father was working in the coal mines, but when work started to slow up, he left and came up to Chicago, where he went into construction work as a laborer. He worked on the construction of buildings like the Merchandise Mart and the old Stevens Hotel, which is now the Conrad Hilton Hotel.

We—the rest of the family—stayed in southern Illinois until the school year was over; then we, too, moved up to the Chicago area. That was in June, 1930.

When I got to Benton, I was fourteen and had already had one year of high school in Scotland. But they advised me to take that freshman year over again. In this little town of Benton I was a novelty—from Scotland, you know, with a Scottish brogue, dressed differently than the American kids. A little shorty going to school with kids that were sixteen and seventeen years old, big six-footers. I felt kind of out of place.

But I didn't mind going to school as a freshman again in Benton, because it was a repetition of everything that I'd already had—especially the French class. The class was using the same book I had used in Scotland. So my French teacher would call on some of the American children to read from this particular book, and when they got stuck, she would call on "Lachlan." It must have been something to hear Lachlan reading French with his Scottish accent.

I did fine that year, but when they uprooted us again and brought us up here to Chicago—where I had to go to Hyde Park High School and where I didn't know a soul—then I had problems. I didn't apply myself. I was a truant. And I did a lot of bad things because I felt out of place.

Actually, I got kicked out of high school. But I was still too young to go to work, and this was during the depression, when jobs were scarce. So I went to Washburn Trade School as a special student. I went five days a week, and I liked it. I was studying electricity. When I reached seventeen or eighteen years and could go to work, then I left school.

The education that I got in Scotland was far superior to the education that I got in America. In a Scottish high school you take more subjects. I was taking algebra and geometry, English, French, Latin, science, and history all at the same time before I left.

While I was still in school, I began going with my father to the bowling green. My father had been a lawn bowler over in Scotland before I was old enough to play, and he had gotten a lot of pleasure out of the game. So when we came to this country, he got me interested in the game.

It wasn't difficult for my father to interest me in lawn bowling. You see, games had been a big part of growing up in Scotland for me. In the summertime it stays light there almost until midnight, so we children could play long after supper. We had all kinds of games, even some that aren't played in this country. We played a game similar to baseball that we called rounders, and we played hide and seek, kick the can, and many others.

And it seemed as if there were seasons for the games. Everybody would be flying kites for a couple of weeks, and then we'd all be spinning tops, and then there would be a session of marble games, and then we'd start playing soccer.

Well, lawn bowling was the game that the men played in Scotland, so it was natural for me to start playing when we came to America and I was old enough. But let me tell you about the game.

Lawn bowling is one of the oldest sports in the world; they say the Romans played it. It has been popular in Scotland since about the tenth or eleventh century. You start with a white ball about the size of a billiard ball, which you roll down a grass alley. Then each player rolls a set of four balls. The object is to roll your four balls so that they will stop as close to the white ball as possible or so that they will move the white ball to your advantage. This is difficult because the balls are weighted on one side; they don't roll straight. The game is counted in a manner similar to the way horseshoes are counted. For example, if I had two of my balls closer to the white ball than any of yours, I would get two points.

When I began to play, years ago, I belonged to a Scottish lawn-bowling club. My Uncle Lachlan and my two cousins, both Lachlans, also belonged to the club. In order to identify us, this is what they did at the club. My father's name was Duncan, so they initialed me L. D. McArthur. One cousin's father was Matthew, so he became L. M. McArthur. My other cousin was the son of Roger McArthur, so he was L. R.

McArthur. And my uncle—he stayed just plain Lachlan McArthur.

By the time I was twenty-one, I had become a pretty good lawn bowler. That was in 1937, when I was working in the steel mills. The national championship was held in Chicago that year, and I led a team consisting of my father and two uncles in the competition. We won the four-man event. And my cousin L. M. teamed up with me to win the doubles.

Now my son is a lawn bowler. When he was twenty, he won first place in the singles competition at the national championship. He and I have played together in competitions, just as I did with my father.

I miss quite a few things about my native country: the food, the scenery, the vacations. The meals in Scotland are very plain—meat, vegetables, and potatoes. But I miss the fish-and-chips, the ice cream, and the pastries. We had a much greater variety of pastries. And I miss the biscuits—we call them cookies here.

I miss being able to go to the seaside and to the hills. And the odors—the wild flowers seemed to have a much stronger odor in Scotland than they do in this country. But every once in a while I get a whiff of something that reminds me of Scotland. When I smell sea fish, that brings back my recollection of Aberdeen, a resort town on the North Sea. We spent one vacation in Aberdeen, and I remember going to the fish market as the boats were coming in to unload the herring and the cod.

I do miss those vacations. For several years my aunt had a farm ten miles from Blantyre, and each year my mother would pack up all of us kids to go to the farm for a couple of weeks. It was supposed to be a vacation. But if you were twelve or thirteen, you could be of use on the farm, you know. So at the crack of dawn they'd get us up. We stood around while all the cows were milked. And then, I remember, I would go with my older cousins to deliver milk—with a horse-drawn wagon. We made two runs: one went into Airdrie, and one went into Coatbridge. Those were two neighboring towns. Well, when we got back, we would have a big breakfast. Then, if it was haying time, we spent the rest of the day out helping to bring in the hay. Or if it was weeding time, we spent the rest of the day going down rows of turnips and pulling weeds. And this was a vacation? But I guess I kind of liked to go out there; it was a change.

I should mention that the island that consists of England, Scotland, and Wales would fit inside the state of Illinois. The differences in distances between Scotland and America are tremendous. We think nothing of picking up and driving a thousand miles on a vacation in this country. But in Scotland, if we went from Blantyre to Glasgow—eight miles on a bus—it was a big deal. Maybe because of the difference in distance, life seems to go at a slower pace in Scotland, even yet.

One thing I don't miss is the weather. Because Scotland is surrounded by water—and even inland you're not too far from the sea—you get a lot of clouds and rain and fog. I may be exaggerating, but it seemed to me that on about 300 days out of the year we'd have rain; maybe not all day, but sometime during the day it would rain. You couldn't plan on a picnic the next Saturday and expect to get good weather; you'd just have to take your chances. The temperature stays pretty much around 40 to 65 degrees all year. But when it gets cold, because the humidity is high, it's a penetrating kind of cold—damp and clammy. To express it in five letters, the weather in Scotland, as I remember it, was l-o-u-s-y.

I'm sure that had I stayed in Scotland, or had my family stayed, I would have been working down in that dirty old coal mine. And there would have been no pleasure attached to that. The tradition was that if a father was a coal miner, his sons were coal miners. My father's father was a coal miner. And all my father's brothers, those who stayed in Scotland, were coal miners, though not all went down into the mines to do the digging. From that angle, I'm sure glad we left.

8

Greek Tragedies

ANDREW YIANNOPOULOS *came to this country with his father in 1913 to work and help support the family back in Greece. He was not quite thirteen.*

At age seventy-six he is a gentle and sensitive man, a self-educated man who loves books and the theater. For some ten years Andrew Yiannopoulos devoted his life to Greek theater in America; he directed his own Greek company, which performed modern Greek plays and the ancient tragedies. The tragedies he regards with a special love.

Several years ago Mr. Yiannopoulos returned to his native Greece, but he was disappointed and disillusioned with what he found. He came back to the United States to live out his life. He had made a discovery: During the past sixty years the United States had become his home.

Andrew Yiannopoulos lives on Chicago's North Side in a large high-rise apartment building, which is owned by a group of Greek-Americans who offer housing to senior citizens. He lives alone and has no immediate family. He says his life is monotonous and lonesome. He is in poor health and walks with difficulty; but sometimes, in conversation, his eyes shine with the intelligence and warmth of a strong spirit. The doorman of the building says Andrew Yiannopoulos is a special kind of person: "We love him here."

I was dreaming the other night that I walked up the mountain to the little village in Greece where I was born. I can't walk from here to the elevator with these calluses on the bottom of my feet, but I was dreaming that I walked up there. It is a very steep mountainside; you always think that you will fall right down into the ravine. The mountain is on one side, all rugged, and the village is on the other side, and in between is a small river. But you don't dare to look down from either side, because if you fall, it's about fifteen hundred feet—two thousand, maybe.

When I was a child, I used to go up that mountain to a little church above our village three or four times a year for the celebration of the Virgin Mary. We had a church up there in her name. And the people from thirty or forty surrounding villages would all walk up there to that church.

My village is very small. When I was a child, about fifty families were living there. Now there are about thirty families. It was named Koutsi, but they've changed the name. During the Second World War it was destroyed by the Germans; the people have rebuilt some of it. By train, it's an hour from Corinth, the biblical town. By mule, as the Greek people used to say, or walking, it was three hours.

When I was young, my father was working in America, and I was going to school. But I helped my mother as much as I could; I worked after school. The farms are not like here, individual farms. The village homes are together in one place, and the homestead is out of the village. Both are on the mountainside. The houses are tilted—just like that. We had a goat for milk, and a donkey, and a horse—a mare. And I used to take care of them, take them to graze. Toward evening when my mother would be through working on the farm, we'd all come together home. I had two sisters and a brother, a baby brother.

By the time my father came back from America—he had been there for five years doing factory and railroad work—I had grown up. I was nine and a half, ten years old. Then I did a little more work. I used to throw stones away from the fields where we plowed for the wheat. Stones were all over. You put them on the side. Dug them up and put them on the side. We had wheat fields, and we had currants. Currants are a small seedless raisin, and they grow around Corinth. During the months of March, April, May, June, and July, we worked in the currants. We plowed the wheat in October and November, and in June we threshed the wheat. Most of the kids left school at nine or ten. But now there is a law; they've got to go to school in Greece, just like here.

Even in Greece my mother was saying, "I'm going to make a professor out of my boy." It sounded funny the way she said it in Greek. And my schoolmaster, he liked me quite a bit—I think because my father was in America. My father was the only one in this country at that time. My schoolmaster helped me as much as he could. He taught me how to be sure to be a good penman, to write straight. He used to scold me when I didn't. Perhaps it's because of them that I wanted to educate myself, to read and to learn.

We had such poverty in Greece. I remember I was always sick while I was living there. I had headaches every three or four days. I don't know whether it was due to malnutrition or the hard work of picking up those stones. I don't know, but I was sick. And as soon as I got on the boat to come to this country, I never had another headache. And another thing: When I was a youngster in Greece, I couldn't eat meat without getting sick. We had a little meat to eat once in a while, but I couldn't eat it. The first meat I ate was in New York—it was forced on me. I thought I wouldn't be able to eat it, but I did. And now, after all these years, I'm back to not eating meat. I can't eat because of my teeth.

After my father returned, he stayed in Greece for a year and a half, and then he brought me back with him to America. For any child, to see America—it was a dream. My teacher said, "Are you sure that you will be happy in the other land?" I said, "Oh yes, sure." I didn't want him to stop me. I promised my father I would work day and night in America to help make a living for the family. "You just take me there," I said. But I was only twelve years old. My father didn't know the laws. He didn't know that I would have to go to school instead in this country. If he had known, maybe I would have never seen America. I'm glad he didn't.

When I was a child, I heard the same thing about America that they hear now: the Land of Golden Opportunity. Yes, well, they have proof: Greeks in the old country had no chance whatever to become anything unless they were the sons and daughters of aristocracy. But when they came here, they worked hard; they got into business; they made money. They raised their families, and their children went to school. You could see the difference in the life for them.

So I came to America with my father. I came in June, 1913. I wasn't yet thirteen, I was but twelve. I went to school in this country for about two years. That's all my father could afford—then I had to start to work. I began to study by myself; I studied books to try to cultivate myself. But in school the fifth grade is as high as I went. I did go to night school to take typing and shorthand, one year of each, but then I couldn't afford to continue with that, either. I began to type, and I would practice writing letters in English to my schoolmates in Greece.

I always loved books; I loved to read. I remember the first thing that I read in English. It was "Hiawatha." I could lose sleep just reciting it. I'd get a picture of the whole thing from beginning to the end—I was in love with it. Minnehaha and Hiawatha. I wrote letters to my school chums in Greece about it, and I told them to find Longfellow translated into Greek so that they could appreciate what I was reading. And then I read about the American Indians, and I felt guilty as a white man for what white men had done to the whole race of Indian people.

My father and I were living in Toledo, Ohio, and working on the railroad. I worked for two years on the road, con-structing the sections, until I was sixteen. When I became sixteen, I started to work as a car checker or yard clerk. I worked in Toledo for about three years. I also worked for the Pennsylvania Railroad. My father was here with me working for eight years, and then he went back to Greece. I stayed.

You see, I had become interested in the theater—Greek theater. And I had gotten involved in a theatrical scheme—producing Greek plays—and lost all my money, including the little bit my father had put in the bank to encourage me to build up. I had saved about $400, and I lost it. My father didn't know about it, and I didn't want to tell him. So when he was ready to go back to Greece, I said, "What's the use in my going to Greece? Greece is at war with Turkey, and they'll take me into the army." I was the only older boy he had, and he consented to let me stay in America. I let him go back to Greece, and then I wrote to him, and I told him about losing the savings. My father, being a common railroad worker, a peasant, valued money quite a bit. He didn't forgive me. He stopped writing to me, and when the Second World War came along, we lost contact. He died during the war, and my mother died right after the war.

I had become interested in theater after I took part in a school production. But there were no stage openings for me. And then I saw my first Greek production in Detroit, where I was working for the Pennsylvania Railroad when a Greek company passed through. I saw that the Greek production was done so poorly, I thought I could do better. I happened to find some amateurs, and we started going to Cleveland, Pittsburgh, and a few small towns in Pennsylvania where there were Greek communities. We gave performances, and I lost every last cent I had. I had to go back to Detroit and go to work as a dishwasher, and then as a waiter in a restaurant. Later there were other theater companies coming from Greece, and I used to help them. They gave me a little pay. I became interested in printing and began to work as a printing salesman. I took orders for the printing of restaurant menus. And that's how I made my living. I'd work part-time in the theater and part-time in printing. For a time, I was directing my own company.

While I was working with one of the theater companies from Greece, I met a girl, and we became engaged. She was a member of one of the companies. But she was here with her relatives, and they went back to Greece. I promised to go back, too, but in the meantime, I had spent all the money that I had. I had to make more money. She died at the beginning of the war, but I didn't know about it until five years later. Her sister wrote to me as soon as the mail began to come from Greece. She wrote that my girl had died. I loved her. I never married after that. Then, too, I was never in a position financially to take care of a wife and home.

I tell you, the Greek theater was important in this—my girl had been in the theater; her family was in the theater. And after she left to go to Greece, I began to attach myself more to the theater, and I found some outlet in giving plays, especially Greek tragedies. I was involved with the Greek theater for about ten years. Something drove me to it. I mean I felt I must keep in touch with my sweetheart. I felt as long as I was working in the theater that my mind, my soul would be in touch with her.

I never made much money in my life; I didn't want to make money, anyhow. I was always afraid of everything connected with money. For instance, I never gambled. I never played cards in my life. Some people were not so careful how they made money, and that was repulsive to me.

When I went back to visit Greece, some of my relatives that had come to this country and made a little money asked me, "How come you were better educated than all of us, and you didn't make any money?" They always thought I had more schooling. I couldn't find an answer. But then, I didn't exactly choose not to make money, either. We had depressions, you know. When I first came here in 1913, there was a depression before the beginning of the First World War, and there was a depression right after the war, and there was the Great Depression in the 1930s—constant depressions. So some of us couldn't make it; others could. Most of the people I knew that came from Greece did not make fortunes, but they made what, for them, was a fortune. They raised their families, and their children became doctors, lawyers, and technicians—professional people. Their parents were proud.

Two years ago I made a visit to my home in Greece. I had intended years before to go back to live, but my dream had vanished when the girl that I loved died. And then, after my mother and father both died, I really didn't even have a desire to go back. But two years ago somebody owed me a little money, and they gave it to me, and I thought, "I'm healthy. Why not go?" I saw my younger brother; he was sixty years old. And my two sisters: one was seventy, and the other one was seventy-two. I hadn't seen them in all those years. I loved my mother, but I don't remember how she looked—it's probably because I left so young. I asked my older sister. She said that she looked exactly like our mother. My sister is very short, shorter than I am. She's about four foot, ten inches tall. My mother had always seemed like a tall woman. I just couldn't make it out.

Greece seemed to have changed very little, at least in the country around my village. Electricity had gone up the mountain where I was born, but there was very little progress otherwise. The houses look the same. They have running water, but the toilet facilities are poor. They still use the old methods of cultivating the land. They thresh wheat by hand; they don't have threshing machines. The people are nice, but they're not educated. Over there in Greece, if you don't agree with them, they won't talk to you the next day.

I had read so much about ancient Greece since I came to this country that I had ancient Greece on my mind. When I left Greece as a child, I didn't know anything about ancient Greek history. I learned all that here. Everything I've learned and forgotten, I've learned and forgotten in this country. But when I went back to visit Greece, I found something completely different from the ancient Greece I had learned about. It was the difference 2,500 years make.

And when I came back to this country, I got sick. My memory failed me; everything else failed me. I got sick with diabetes and phlebitis. I went to the hospital, and what little money I had left from my trip, I spent with doctors.

And finally I came to this institution. I pay the rent and cook for myself. It's a very monotonous life. But the people here are wonderful—most are Jewish.

I've got plenty wrong with me. I can't eat meat. People don't understand why I can't eat meat; they knew me just a few years ago when I used to eat meat very heavy. With the last operation I lost twenty-five pounds, and the teeth don't fit anymore. And I have calluses on my right foot under my toes so bad that I can't walk. And since the doctors forbid me to use salt, everything is tasteless; even bread is tasteless. You're too young to tell you that I'm anxious to die, but that's how I feel.

I didn't decide to become an American citizen until I got to Greece, and then I wrote back to my lawyer that I want to become a citizen. I came back to this country; I'll die in this country and be buried here. America has been my home for sixty years. I feel that if I'm going to be buried in this country, I want to be a citizen. I don't want to be buried in Greece. Nothing connects me with Greece, now that I have seen it again. I had had an idea of Greece in my mind all those years, and when I went to Greece, I found something different. But because I left this country to go back, I have to wait two more years yet before I can become an American citizen. If I'm alive, that's my last hope—the last wish I have to fulfill.

9

But, My Goodness,
Is This America?

Rockford, Illinois, is a city with a large Swedish-American population. There EDITH SVENSSON EDGREN *lives alone in a white frame house filled with beautiful furniture made by her late husband, who was a cabinetmaker.*

Her parents died young, and when Edith was six, she was separated from her younger brother and sister. She went to live with an aunt and uncle, and her brother and sister went to live with her mother's cousin. Edith's new family was not so prosperous as her brother's and sister's; so when she was fourteen, she began to do live-in housework. By the time she came to America in 1920, she had been on her own for seven years. Edith was twenty-one; her brother, who made the trip with her, was sixteen.

She remembers her brother with fondness—especially for the "crazy times" they had together on their way to the new country. Unlike Edith, he went on to school in America and eventually earned a doctorate. For more than thirty years he worked as a photographer in Rockford, having learned the trade from his Swedish-American uncle. Edith settled in Rockford, married, and raised a family. She has visited Sweden only once since she left, and that visit was made nearly fifty years ago.

Edith is a spunky woman, an excellent storyteller with a keen sense of humor. After talking with Edith for a while, a listener comes to anticipate the rise in her voice that signals a humorous observation.

I always thought that I would go to America because I had my aunts here, my father's sisters. They always wrote that we should come. You know, people who would come home to Sweden from America, they would brag. They said that America was so-o-o wonderful. Oh, you know, nothing but like gold and silver. Well, I never believed that because I tell you one thing: If my aunts had been so rich, why didn't they ever send us anything? Well, that's the way it was.

My brother came with me. He had listened to two men bragging about how wonderful it was in America, you know. He had such a good home; he should never have left it. But he was young, and he thought it was going to be so nice. My aunt in Sweden didn't want him to go, but he got so impressed with these two men talking, so—

We came with a Danish boat. *King Oskar,* they called it. King Oskar must have been a Danish king. It took us eleven days coming over. We had a terrible storm. That was in October. It was so stormy that we couldn't go out on the deck, you know, for five days. The water just swept over the deck of the boat, and there was a man who was working his way over to America, and it took him. They never found him. It just swept him overboard. I didn't know him.

They never told anybody, but I got acquainted with the boy who served the food, and the last day I asked him. "There was a little commotion," I said. "Was anybody hurt or anything?" He told me that the man had just disappeared and that there was nothing they could do because there was too much storm.

This boat had been one that they used to carry livestock to different countries. And they fixed it over for people. Well, I thought there was kind of a funny smell to it. But it was all fixed up where we had our cabins. There were so many people who came over that year. The boats were all filled up. And then there was this boat, and we took it.

They put the Swedish people on one part of the boat and the Polish people on another. We went through the Polish section. They were lying on the floor packed together like sardines, and they were throwing up. It was a mess. They had bags. I think you could throw up in bags.

I was never seasick. I never threw up. So I used to take food down to the other ones who were sick but could eat a little bit.

The food wasn't bad. It was all right. We always had coffee in the afternoon, and some rolls. No fancy things, but there was good food. It was brought from Sweden.

My aunt thought we wouldn't get enough food on the boat. She thought it was like in the olden days when my uncle's brother went to America, about sixty or seventy years back. She thought it was the same thing, you know. And so she had sent all kinds of food. She had sent smoked sausage with. She had sent cheese with. But we got enough to eat on the boat, and my aunt's food got all green and larvy. I had to drown it all in the ocean.

And, oh yes, I had six little bottles that she had sent with. Five were juice and one was whiskey. I remember another girl and me, we got very chummy on the boat. Neither of us could sleep at night because of the noise of the motor. It sounded like a threshing machine. So she used to take one little "klunk" out of that whiskey, and I took one. And we went to sleep, you know. We just took a little bit, and we got so dizzy. We weren't used to it. And so we went to sleep.

You weren't supposed to take whiskey on the trip. At Copenhagen we had to open up our suitcases. And the inspector asked me what was in the bottles. "Oh, that's juice," I said. I didn't think I'd tell him one was whiskey. He must have looked in all of them but two, and one was the whiskey. So that was all right.

But my brother had a bottle of cognac that was supposed to be the best in Sweden; my mother's cousin had sent that to my uncle in America. My brother had to pay a fine.

My aunt had sent a knife and fork, too. The official stuck his finger on the fork. Oh, he swore, and he was mad. I couldn't help laughing, but I didn't dare show it to him. I thought he was kind of nosy.

I was supposed to take care of my brother because he was sixteen years old. He was awful hard to take care of because he wanted to see so many things. So we had some crazy times. He thought he was a man, you know.

I remember the first day we got on the boat, he got seasick. He was white as a ghost, and I said, "Are you sick?" Oh, no, he said, he wasn't sick. And then he went over to the railing there and threw up, and he came back. "You were sick," I said. "No!" he said. He wouldn't admit it, but he was standing there throwing up over the railing. Wasn't that terrible? Yeah, that was funny.

I used to tell him once in a while what trouble I had with him, and he never wanted to hear it. He was a very nice man.

118

He was a wonderful man. Course, he's dead now; he died a year ago. But he sure was good to me, and to everybody else.

When we got to New York, there was a crazy thing. The steamship company sent out a lady. She was supposed to help us—see that we got something to eat and got to the right railroad station. She wasn't Swedish. She couldn't speak Swedish, and she couldn't speak English. Why in the world should they have hired her? There were sixteen of us from Sweden who were going to take different trains. She told us to follow her, and we followed, all right.

We were going to have coffee, and she took up money. She took fifty cents from every single one. That donut and coffee, I found out later, wasn't more than twenty-nine cents. She stole the rest of that money.

And then we all wanted to send telegrams. My brother was sitting with a man in another place, and she took a telegram from him, too. She took telegrams from both me and my brother. I couldn't make her understand that she should only take one from us. I don't remember how much money she took. I thought my aunt would get two telegrams, but she never got a single one.

I must say, I really didn't like it when I first came here. See, I had worked in Gothenburg, and we had all the modern conveniences. In Sweden we had so much water, and we used it to make electricity. My aunt in Rockford still had gas lamps in her house. They didn't have electricity yet.

And as we came into Rockford there was a little station—I guess it wasn't being used—and the pigeons were flying out of the windows. I said to my brother, "But, my goodness, is this America?" "Yeah, I suppose so," he said. I almost felt terrible when I saw those pigeons. You know, the little stations in Sweden were painted and nice, and everything was so clean. You never saw pigeons flying up.

It was so terrible hot here, too. I didn't feel good from that heat. I remember that I weighed 145 pounds when I came to Rockford, and after my first summer here I weighed less than 100 pounds. I didn't like the food, either. I was a pretty good cook, and in Sweden the people I worked for were rich and could afford to have good food. Very good food.

I came to my Aunt Ingrid, and, course, she was kind of poor. She had broken her arm, and my uncle had been let off from work. And there was not much work to be had here in America in 1920 and 1921.

It cost $102 one way for the boat from Copenhagen to New York, and the rest of the trip you had to pay for, too. Aunt Ingrid had sent me some of the money. I don't know whether they borrowed it or not. I paid them back. They were, like I said, poor; they needed it. I paid them twenty dollars a month for the room and board, and then, well, they got almost every cent for a year.

I felt kind of sorry for my aunt because she couldn't do anything with that broken arm. She couldn't even comb her own hair. So I did her housework, and I worked at the stocking factory. I tell you, I didn't have it easy. I had to support them, too. I made only twenty-five cents an hour. Everybody made only twenty-five cents an hour in the factory. You put the tops of stockings, cotton stockings, on with a machine, and you really had to have good eyes to do that.

I couldn't speak English at all when I came. I went to night school for a little while, but I couldn't go very long because one night a week I had to rub [wash] the clothes. And in the morning I'd have to get up early and wring out the wash, and then hang it up. My aunt had no washing machine. I had to warm the iron on the stove. Even in Sweden we had electric irons. And then I always had to help my aunt with the cooking, wash the dishes, and mend the clothes. I sewed all our clothes, my clothes and her clothes. So I was always busy.

But I wasn't homesick or frightened. I had been out working—in Sweden, you know—and, well, I was just used to being on my own. So I wasn't homesick or anything. But I just didn't like it. I really didn't like it.

They didn't want me to go anywhere. They treated me like I was a little girl ten years old. They were going to tell me what to do. And I wasn't used to that. They could never see that I was grown up. I had to grow up young.

I didn't want to be rude. I was brought up that you shouldn't be rude to old people. I didn't want to say anything. I thought: I can't stay here anyway. And my aunt was getting better in her arm and could help herself. My uncle could scrub the floors and things like that.

I had been in America more than a year, and I didn't have more than forty dollars left over. Course, my aunt borrowed that, too, when I left. I was kind of bare.

But I was never sorry that I came to America. Now they have it wonderful in Sweden, but in those days they didn't. If you were going to work for your living, it was easier to work for your living here than in Sweden. I had always wanted to be a nurse, but that cost money in Sweden. You had to go to school, and my aunt and uncle didn't have that kind of money. So I could never do that. The only thing I could do was housework. But I loved to cook. I loved to cook—I did like that.

So I went to work doing housework. You had your room and board free, and then I made nine dollars a week. It was better to do housework in America than in Sweden, in a way. You could make more money here when you went to live with the families and worked for them. And you worked so much harder in Sweden. They expected lots more of you. I just felt I could do better here than in Sweden.

At first I worked for Swedish people. They were nice. But I didn't learn much English—my aunt couldn't talk very much English, and these people talked Swedish an awful lot. So I thought I had better go to work for a family that talked English. I was with the Swedish family only six months. It was easy to get jobs doing housework because the families all wanted Swedish girls. I guess they thought the Swedish girls were used to more work.

Then my aunt died seven or eight years after I came to America. I went back to Sweden for a while then, but I haven't been back since. I have a sister there, you know. I should go. She writes me often. But after you've got your children, and they've married, and you've been here for a while, you could never go back to stay. But it would be nice to visit.

My husband always said we should go for a visit, but then he got sick, and there was no reason to go. But I may yet. You never know. I could go for a month. They say don't go for any longer than six weeks. Your relatives get tired of you, and you get tired of them.

I have arthritis now, and that gives me a lot of trouble, especially if I'm on my feet for a long time. I can't walk far outside. I do all right inside. I'm just an old lady. But I still love to cook. Sometimes I stand in there and cook for myself, and I think, "Why in the world did I cook all that food, when I'm just here alone?"

10

Bad Times
Before the Union

MORRIS GORDON *was only twelve when he came to America
with his fifteen-year-old sister in 1907. Both of their parents
had died. They came from the Russian Ukraine to live with an
uncle in Chicago, and Morris immediately went to work for a
clothing manufacturer, Hart Schaffner & Marx. He worked
there for the next forty-seven years.*

*In Morris's early days in the United States, the unions were
just beginning to organize in the clothing industry. Morris
worked for three years without union representation. It was, he
says, a bad time.*

*Then, in 1910, some 40,000 clothing workers in Chicago went
on strike. They sought shorter working hours, more pay,
improved working conditions—and union representation. It
was a long, violent strike, but in the end Hart Schaffner &
Marx signed a contract with the union—the only clothing
manufacturer in Chicago to do so that year.*

*Morris Gordon was one of the strikers. Having joined the
Amalgamated Clothing Workers of America in 1911, he is now
one of the union's oldest members. Morris served a two-year
term as president of Amalgamated's Samuel Levin Center for
Retired Members after he retired in 1957. For the past seven*

years he has been the center's custodian. As custodian, he sells tickets to various functions, answers the phone, takes visitors on tours of the center, and talks to groups of children. He seldom misses a day at the center; he's the first to arrive and the last to leave.

Morris's wife, whom he married in 1917, died a few years ago; but his two daughters take turns bringing meals and shopping for him. One daughter lives in Chicago, one in a suburb. He has two grandchildren and seven great-grandchildren.

Morris is a man of slight build, and his back is permanently bent from his years of work as a tailor. He shows no tolerance for unnecessary words and speaks slowly and distinctly. His eyes shine with amusement at being interviewed.

I was an orphan in the old country. I come from Russia. I was born in 1895 in a small village in the Ukraine. When I was four years old, my father passed away; and when I was eleven, my mother passed away. After they died, I went to work for a tailor, and that's where I learned my trade. I worked for one year, and then I came to this country.

In Russia when I was young, I saw a lot of Jewish people getting killed, a lot of people getting beat up, a lot of looting—you know, taking from Jewish people. It was called a *pogrom*. We had a lot of pogroms—almost every month, I think. Well, this is something that I have to tell you. You see, the place where I worked, my boss was also Jewish, but he lived in a non-Jewish house. I used to go on errands for the landlady, and she would put a cross around my neck. And nobody bothered me. They thought I was a Christian.

In the old country I had a Jewish teacher, and I had a

Russian teacher that used to come to the house to teach me—a private teacher. My mother didn't want me to go to the school that Jews were allowed to go to, so she hired a private teacher. When I came to this country, I couldn't go to school because I had to work. I couldn't go to night school after work because I took work home with me in the evenings. I worked all the time. And then, after I joined the union, I was a good union member and I was busy at the union headquarters. But still I taught myself. I know how to read, and I know how to write.

I started to work at Hart Schaffner & Marx, a clothing factory in Chicago, in 1907, as soon as I arrived in this country. I did handwork. I was twelve years old. It was illegal for me to work in a factory at that age, but the foreman of the shop told me that I should tell the inspectors, when they came around, you know, that I was fifteen.

We had to be at work by seven-thirty in the morning and work until six in the evening, and on Saturday from seven-thirty to one. I worked fifty-four hours a week, and they gave me work to take home. I made seven dollars a week, plus twenty cents an hour for the work I did at home.

I was happy to make a living, there was nobody to support me. I lived with my uncle, and I paid him three dollars a week for room and board.

I worked at Hart Schaffner & Marx for three years without the union. It was a bad time. Before the union, we were treated like animals. You couldn't do this; you couldn't do that. If you talked to one another, they used to tell you to stop talking. You know, they were afraid that we were going to get organized—to start a union.

Most of the workers were foreigners. We had people from

all countries: Russians, Italians, Polish, Bohemians, even a few Swedes, too. Next to me was an Italian man. I couldn't talk to him; he couldn't talk to me—we spoke different languages. That's the way they arranged us. They wouldn't put me next to a Russian because they thought we'd start talking.

What can I tell you? You see, everything was made by hand in that time. They used to press clothes with a 24-pound gas press. Some of those presses used to scorch the suits, and the bosses would charge us for the whole suit—fifteen dollars a suit. And we went home without pay.

I worked on the fifth floor, and you had to walk up all the way. No elevators. And it was hot with those presses. It used to get 80 and 90 degrees in the summer. They never had a fan. And we had no breaks—only lunchtime, three-quarters of an hour.

And the sanitary facilities: three hundred people on one floor, and only one washroom for men *and* women. One towel on the roller. But after the strike in 1910, the working conditions started to change for the better.

The strike wasn't really planned. But—well, I knew that something was going to happen. I knew that. It was Bessie Hillman, Sidney Hillman's wife, that called the strike. Sidney Hillman later became president of the Amalgamated Clothing Workers of America. But he was a clothing worker, like me, in those days. You see, Bessie worked in another section, and they were getting starvation wages. I don't remember exactly what they got, but it couldn't have been more than seven dollars a week—that was considered a lot of money. But you had to be a fast worker to make seven dollars a week by the piece.

Anyway, she called the strike and led the workers out of the shop. Her name was Abramowitz then, Bessie Abramowitz. That was her maiden name. She and Hillman were married later; I remember the wedding.

Bessie must have been about eighteen or nineteen years old at the time of the strike. She and the other strikers had whistles. And they went around to all the shops blowing their whistles—that was a sign that the strike had started. When the workers heard the whistles, everybody came out. I remember that we walked out as soon as we heard the whistles. We had 40,000 people out on strike—clothing workers from all the shops in Chicago.

The strike lasted eighteen weeks. I still remember that we were starving. They used to give us meal tickets, you know. They had made arrangements with a restaurant to give us lunch for a ticket. We were supported by the American Federation of Labor and by the head of the union—what was his name—Gompers, Samuel Gompers. They gave us a lot of help. They used to buy the meal tickets and distribute them among the strikers. Jane Addams used to go out and collect money for the strikers, and we used to have meetings at Hull House. She helped us a lot. She was a nice lady—nice to talk to. And then that criminal lawyer—I forgot his name. The famous one. Clarence Darrow. He helped us. He used to come and make speeches. He was a good speaker; I heard him. But I didn't know him. I was afraid of lawyers.

I didn't have to live on one meal a day. I was living with my sister at that time, and I ate over there. She was a clothing worker, too, but she was married. I remember that the strike wasn't going so good, you know, and there was a rumor going around that the American Federation of Labor was going to give us a strike benefit—pay us for being in the strike. So all of us, all the strikers, walked down to the Board of Trade Building on LaSalle Street, where they had their offices. But it was a false rumor. And the police started to chase us. They were mounted police, and at that time the police horses were trained to knock you down. Now, you know, you can picket; you can do almost anything. But then we couldn't pass out leaflets to other nonunion workers at other places. We couldn't do this; we couldn't do that. It was all illegal—even picketing. You could be arrested. When you walked the picket line, you were putting your life in danger.

There was a lot of trouble during the strike. Two were killed, two workers on the picket line. They were fighting with the scabs, some of the people who were working in place of the workers on strike. I knew them, the ones who were killed. I walked the picket line. Once I was arrested, but I wasn't hurt.

I remember in that 1910 strike, somebody donated Saturday's papers to the strikers. We should go out and sell the papers. So I went out on a Saturday, and I brought in twenty dollars from selling papers and gave it to Hillman. And Hillman looked at my shoes. He says, "Man, you need a new pair of shoes." He took out four dollars and gave it to me —says, "Go buy yourself a pair of shoes."

That's the story of the strike. Only one company—Hart Schaffner & Marx—signed a contract that year; but by 1915 all the clothing manufacturers in Chicago had signed up.

I was a steward in the shop for three or four years. I practically can't remember—it was back so long ago. I used to collect dues and take complaints. The complaints I would take back to the union office, so that they should take care of them. There were plenty of complaints. But the main complaint was money: The workers wanted more money.

Now the union doesn't have any trouble collecting dues, but then we did. One time I was collecting dues, and the foreman comes over to me and says that I can't do it. I says, "I'm going to do it."

"Well," he says, "don't get sassy. I'm telling you to stop."

"I'm not going to stop," I says.

So he gave me a suspension. I went to Hillman, and he tells me, "*I'm* going to keep you out for two weeks." I stayed out, and I got paid for it. They took my case to the arbitration board. After that I didn't have any trouble collecting dues.

It was bad before the union, and it was bad during the depression in the 1930s. I was making about three dollars a week. We worked maybe two hours a day at the most. But they kept us on. I used to go in every day. My wife and I lost a building, but during the depression we had saved a few dollars that we managed to hold on to, and I opened a cleaning store—cleaning and tailoring. And you know, the first week I made a ninety-dollar profit—that was good. So my wife used to take care of the store during the day, and I used to work at Hart Schaffner & Marx. At night, I'd work at the store, and I made pretty good. We had the store for twenty-eight years.

I worked almost fifty years in one place—Hart Schaffner & Marx—and now I'm retired. I used to travel, but I gave that up two years ago when my wife died. I'm too old to travel. I was a precinct captain in my precinct for twelve years, but I gave that up, too—about a year ago. I'm too old to climb steps. But I come here to the center, Amalgamated's Samuel Levin Center for Retired Members, every day. I don't miss a day.

131

11

Helping the Sun to Set on the King's Dominion

DENIS GOULDING *was born February 4, 1893, in County Kerry, Ireland, in the small town of Knockanure, which means "hill of the yew tree." When he was sixteen, Denis joined the IRA, the Irish Republican Army, to fight for his country's independence from Britain. The Irish people had been ruled by Britain— against their will and often inhumanely—since the twelfth century.*

For seventeen years Denis fought in the IRA, sometimes using guns, sometimes words, in what is called the Anglo-Irish War. He survived two hunger strikes and several years as a political prisoner. Although he himself was never injured, he saw many of his friends killed in warfare, tortured in prison, or executed.

Irish representatives finally signed a peace treaty with Britain in 1921, but they signed under Britain's threat of "immediate and terrible war." The treaty included a provision that called for the partition of Ireland into two countries: the Irish Free State, which later became the Republic of Ireland, and Northern Ireland. The Irish Free State, four-fifths of Ireland, would govern itself as a member of the British Commonwealth, but Northern Ireland would remain under British rule.

After the Anglo-Irish War and two years of civil war, Denis Goulding was released from prison, where he had spent fifty-two days on a hunger strike. He returned to Knockanure. Seeing his country divided, he was broken in heart and spirit. He felt he could do no more. Vowing never to return as long as the Union Jack (the British flag) was allowed to fly over any part of his homeland, Denis left Ireland.

On October 26, 1926, he arrived in the United States, where another struggle for independence from British rule had once been fought. He came to make a new home and is now an American citizen.

Denis follows closely the events in Northern Ireland. He passionately supports the IRA's current activities, which he views as a continuation of the struggle in which he participated—a struggle for a free and unified Ireland.

He has never returned to his native country.

It was very few people that wanted to accept the challenge to fight for Ireland's independence. I remember that I accepted that challenge because I was taught my country's history in a farmer's barn, one side of a hedgerow, by an Irishman who did love his country.

We weren't allowed to learn Irish history or geography in what they called the national schools—the regular schools controlled by the British. We had to learn it from the Hedge schoolmasters in underground schools, Hedge schools.

It was very few parents that allowed their children to go to the Hedge schoolmaster for fear of the authorities of the town. They wanted peace. But it happened that my family didn't look at it that way. Generations before me had faced the same fight, the same problem. There are Irish families that have always fought for Ireland's independence down through the centuries. My family, the Goulding family, is among them. So they didn't object to any teacher teaching me Irish history.

One time when we were going to the national schools, we learned that the sun never sets on the king's dominion, that is, the British Empire. That was our education: The sun never sets on the king's dominion. Well, we were determined that it *would* set.

I joined the IRA, the Irish Republican Army, when I was, oh, about sixteen. At first our policy was passive resistance. We organized protest meetings. We got people out together in the nearest town, no matter what the reason—a national celebration or whatever. And there is where you had speakers to protest the existence of an army of occupation in a land that didn't want them.

But we found out that we'd have to prove that we were ready to lay our lives down for what we wanted. And that's what drove us to obtain arms and to train ourselves in guerrilla warfare. That was not an easy job. We were all young, in our twenties at the very most.

I had many different jobs in the IRA, but for a time I was a captain, a staff captain. It was an awfully tiring life. We never had enough to eat; we never had enough sleep. Never. Not for months and months. But still we lived through it. We had very exciting times, *very* exciting times. My family never knew where I was, and neither did anybody else. I was just here today and gone next morning. And nobody knew where or when or what. It didn't profit anybody to know where you had gone and what you were doing.

We were a very closely knit army. There was no getting

away from that fact. We didn't take any monkey business. If you talked loosely, you died. In the circumstances of that time, it was useless if you didn't have discipline, rigid discipline—too many lives depended on it.

It was in the 1918 elections in the county of Waterford that we proved to Britain that we could defeat her at the ballot box. After years of passive and armed resistance, our political party—we were known as Republicans—had become Ireland's dominant party.

The son of an old Irish party man who had attended the British Parliament for many years was put up against one of our men, an IRA man, a Republican. The son was highly decorated from the First World War. He was a good man. He was a young fellow about our age. But he figured his daddy was right, and we figured we were right. We wanted to govern our land for ourselves.

We were never so tired in our lives. We spent twenty days without sleep, it seemed, or with very little sleep. Twenty-five of us—that's all that was there—went day and night from house to house. We told the people we could give them fair play, give them what they had wanted all their lives —freedom. We guaranteed that no Irishman would be conscripted into England's army again. 'Twas legwork all the way.

On the morning of October 26, 1918, the ballot booths were open for voting. And on the tops of the houses, behind chimneys, we saw machine guns for the first time. And British soldiers behind the guns. Huge posters were all over the place: "We're here to protect you so that you can go to the polls to vote." But they were really there to terrify the people, so that they would not go to the polls to vote.

136

And so we had to go from house to house in the early morning hours before daybreak and tell the people: "Don't go until we call for you. We'll send men for you. We'll take you to the polls."

We won hands down. Their man was badly defeated; our man was elected. Six weeks after that, in every part of Ireland—north, south, east, west—our men were elected. We won 73 of Ireland's 105 seats in the British Parliament in the 1918 elections. But instead of going to London to join the British Parliament, our representatives met in Dublin, Ireland. And on January 21, 1919, they declared Ireland an independent republic.

But the British government refused to recognize it as such. Warfare continued. And so our leadership, IRA leadership, decided to send about fifty of us over to Britain to tell the British people of our cause. We thought maybe they could influence their government to negotiate with us. I was one of those fifty young men.

We could go into any English pub, or tavern, and we'd have a crowd around us asking questions. Nobody was insulted when we got through, because they realized that we were telling the truth and that we had the guts to stand up for what we believed.

England, you see, wanted to keep Ireland as her kitchen garden—to supply cheap food to maintain her high industrial output. She discouraged the building of industrial plants in Ireland. For many years Ireland had raised and educated her children only to send them to England to glut the labor market. England wanted our cheap labor to keep her ships sailing to foreign ports with manufactured goods.

But after World War I, England began to feel pressure from

her own people regarding her treatment of Ireland. Those of us who traveled around England helped in that. So in 1921 England's prime minister, Lloyd George—known as the Wizard of Wales—was forced to sue for a truce in Ireland.

Hostilities ceased. An Irish delegation was sent to London to arrange for the orderly removal of occupation forces and to agree on a just compensation for the destruction British forces had wrought in Ireland. But the Wizard had planned quite a surprise.

Lloyd George had written up his own dictation to the Irish people. He set up a boundary line across northeast Ireland and insisted that the six counties above the line would continue to be governed by England. He demanded British use of all Irish ports for a number of years and the completion of payments for lands we had taken back from English landlords. And he threatened "immediate and terrible war" if the Irish delegates did not sign this treaty.

The Irish people were divided over the treaty; the IRA was divided. The majority believed that even though the treaty called for a divided Ireland, the country could be reunited constitutionally within a couple of years. Those of us who knew Irish history knew that Britain would never permit it, but we were in the minority.

A choice had to be made at the polling booths: If the Irish people accepted the treaty without reservation, they would achieve a permanent peace, Lloyd George said; if not, immediate and terrible war. The delegates had no choice but to sign. The Irish people had no choice, either. No people ever voted *for* war, especially a war within their own borders.

We weren't getting our Ireland; we were getting only a part of Ireland, and a part of Ireland is no Ireland. Now, in the War of Independence here in the United States, what if the British government had demanded a fifth of the colonies? What would our answer have been? Well, that is what they demanded in Ireland: a fifth of a little fatherland that's only about the size of the state of Illinois.

My comrades and I, although we were a minority, refused to accept the partition. We knew we couldn't possibly win a war against England in a divided Ireland, but we wanted to protest with our own blood; we wanted a future generation fighting for the freedom of Northern Ireland to be able to tell the world that we never accepted the treaty.

So the next thing we had was civil war—brother fighting brother. Divide and conquer—that's how Lloyd George thought he could win. But fifty years later we find the Irish Republican Army again denying England the right to rule in any part of Ireland.

The provisional government, the so-called Irish Free State government, passed a law imposing the death penalty on anyone carrying arms against that government. My life was in danger twenty-four hours a day. Nobody would have believed that the new government would dare to execute the very men who had fought so hard for Ireland's independence. But they did. They executed seventy-six of my comrades. Finally our commander in chief, Eamon de Valera, ordered us to lay down our arms and let ourselves be taken as prisoners.

And I was taken prisoner—a prisoner of the so-called Free State government. Let me tell you about prison. In a pitch-dark cell you don't hear a noise—not a twitter, not a sound. Oh, it is deadly, unless you sincerely believe in the justice of God and ask Him to help you.

There's such a thing in the Catholic Church as the fourteen Stations of the Cross. I don't know if you're acquainted with what they are. They commemorate the suffering that Christ endured on his way to Calvary from the hall where he was sentenced. Well, on that awful wall in my cell, I had all them stations mapped out in my imagination. I said them stations, and they gave me peace of mind. Nothing scared me. I didn't care what came along. That was the truth.

I spent fifty-two days on a hunger strike in Currah Military Camp in Kildare while I was a prisoner of the so-called Irish Free State. They said they'd turn us loose if we signed surrender papers stating that we wouldn't take up arms, and so on and so on and so on—give them our blessing if they wanted it—and so on. There were 1,400 of us; that's all. But we were determined that we'd die before we'd put our signatures to any paper of that kind.

I had decided what I would do and what I wouldn't do a long time before. I remember, oh, I guess maybe I was eight or nine years old. It was before the First World War—about 1908, somewhere in there. Britain started releasing political prisoners from western Australia. That's where they had the salt mines, and that's where the Irish political prisoners slaved. There was one man, an Irish revolutionary hero, O'Donovan Rossa; he was a big man, but he was bent over. My dad put me on something so that I could see him coming up the street. The man had spent so many years laboring in the salt mines that his back got bent. He had a hard time raising his head to have a look at you.

Well, I remember at the time, and later, I made the remark that I wouldn't slave: I'd die. They'd have to kill me before I'd do it. I'd die of hunger; that's what I'd do. But they didn't conceive of a hunger strike in them days. 'Twas only in our times that we used the hunger strike. If you couldn't defend yourself in any other way, the hunger strike was the last resort.

Hunger is the cruelest weapon a man can use in his defense. The first three days are dreadful. Your body starts to use whatever fat is left on you, and your stomach seems to get disgusted with that. Although there is nothing in your stomach, you can't stop retching. And that goes on for maybe nine days. But from then on it isn't so bad. At least I didn't feel it was so bad. I could have stayed there forever. Course, I was slowly dying—dying of starvation.

I remember when we were set free. An officer came in to me—I was in an isolation cell—and he says, "I'm glad it's over. You're free." Oh, no, I didn't pay any attention to him. I couldn't possibly believe that. Finally he went out and got a newspaper to show me.

Well, I was able to stand up and walk. But when they took me to a hospital, I looked in the mirror and saw that I was completely emaciated. The bones were just barely covered with skin. And, man oh man, we got the best treatment in the world. The nurses were hovering around us twenty-four hours a day. They were scared to death that somebody would die at the last minute.

No man can describe the feelings of dismay and depression that overwhelmed us after we were released from prison and saw our country partitioned, with a ten-foot high, double-row barbed wire fence with guard watchtowers along the line of separation.

At the time, the best of young Irish fellows, the cream of any land, left Ireland. But there were some who stayed behind, too; and from them comes whatever is working in the north of Ireland today. I believe that—truly believe that.

I'd like to be able to say that I'd stayed in Ireland to fight to the end to free all of Ireland. But I wanted to make my own living; I wanted peace just as well as anybody. I knew I wouldn't have it in Ireland because I knew that by nature I couldn't stay quiet.

So I came to this country about two years after my release, on October 26, 1926, with a girl who is now my wife of almost forty years. We sailed on the steamship *Franconia,* and nine days later we landed in New York. I came to make a living and to have peaceable circumstances in which to make that living.

My future wife's sister, who had come to the United States about a year before, lived in Kansas City, Missouri; so we headed out there. Work was all-important, but it was hard to find. I worked that winter for a dairy farmer near Independence, Missouri, and the next spring I went to work in Kansas City for a small steel products company.

Labor unions were not effective in those days; men were hired and fired at will. I was lucky—I didn't get fired. But work finally slacked down to two days a week.

About this time my future wife had gone to see some friends in St. Louis. She wrote back saying her friends thought they could find a better job for me there. So I quit my job in Kansas City and headed for St. Louis in 1927. But the job didn't materialize, and I spent anxious weeks walking and walking, following false rumors, and getting the same frustrating reply—"You are not a citizen"—which I knew by then to be a patent evasion of the truth. The depression was starting then, and there just wasn't any work.

Finally, through acquaintances I found work in University City, a nice clean little suburb of St. Louis in St. Louis County. I belonged to a street repair gang. My wife, Kitty, and I were married about this time—April, 1928.

On the national scene, Herbert Hoover beat Al Smith for the presidency, and the Ford Motor Company electrified the whole country by declaring that its basic wage would be $4 for an eight-hour day—about $25 for a six-day week. A four-room apartment, unheated, cost $25 a month. A job at Ford spelled "gold mine."

My brother-in-law worked at Ford at that time, and he believed he could get me a job. It meant good pay and no trouble with bad weather; so I quickly decided, yes, back to Kansas City again. But would you believe it? The day I disposed of our furniture and bought a bus ticket for Kansas City, a big bunch of workers, my brother-in-law included, were laid off from Ford. Four dollars a day gone.

President Hoover was not the culprit during our Great Depression. It wasn't until the banks closed down in 1929 that Congress finally believed that we were in a depression, even though millions of workers knew it at least one year earlier.

In 1935 Congress passed legislation called the Works Progress Administration, the WPA, which was designed to put people on public improvement jobs at pay decidedly lower than the prevailing industrial wage. I worked for WPA. Some of it was useful work. But some of it was degrading and humiliating work for men who wanted to work to earn a decent living.

By this time we were into President Roosevelt's regime, and Senator Wagner of New York wrote some very useful and badly needed social laws; but all those laws did not produce more employment. It was the Second World War and Hitler that sent us all to work—men, women, and even children.

I came to Chicago in the fall of 1937 and went to work for the Chicago and Western Indiana Railroad as a night policeman protecting traffic at railroad crossings and guarding loaded freight cars from looters. Sometimes we had a little excitement, but generally it was monotonous work—all night, ten hours a night, seven nights a week. During the shorter days of winter and early spring I seldom saw daylight. After four or five years of that, I went to work for the Catholic Archdiocese of Chicago as a maintenance engineer. That's where I worked until 1964, when I retired at the age of seventy-one.

We thank our God and the people of the United States for the opportunity to make a fairly decent living and to raise a good family. Our firstborn, a girl, died in childbirth. We have three sons, one adopted, and they are all in managerial positions in the construction industry. We have fourteen grandchildren. Some have started in college. We hope they will contribute generously to the social structure of *their* native land.

I believe the most valuable product of any land is its youth. I saw what youth could do in my native land. Who would believe that generation after generation would shed their blood for the freedom of their country when the odds seemed impossible? But they did, and they did it gladly.

As a youth in Ireland, I was put through the mill. You'd be surprised at the ideas and the questions that come to you while you're in solitary confinement. You have plenty of time

144

to meditate. And after some of my experiences in my adopted land, I have some questions. Why is it that today we have no money for useful employment, but tomorrow we have plenty of money for destruction? Why is it that municipalities all over our country have no money to pay their employees, while certain segments of our economy reap plentiful harvests? Why is it that humans have to scrounge in city slums in this country to find a living? What is it with our Congress? What is it with our money system?

I think that one of our biggest problems in this country is that we have deliberately robbed our children of the right to know and the duty to obey, through conscience, the laws of a supreme God. I believe that the myth of separation of church and state should be buried and that we should stop robbing our children of the most valuable ingredient in education—a religious belief.

I have something else that I want to say. Not long ago the president of the Republic of Ireland spoke to the Congress of the United States to protest the aid that some Irish-Americans were sending his opposition in Ireland. His opposition, the Sinn Fein party—an old and established party whose leaders have spent their lives and fortunes in the service of Ireland, especially a united Ireland—immediately applied for visas to come to the U.S. to answer the charges against them. But they were refused.

You don't know the frustration and humiliation I felt as an Irish-American when my adopted land refused to admit representatives of my native land. I say to my adopted land, "You called Ireland your friend in 1776. What do you call her today?"

I am now an American citizen, but Ireland is still my native land. I have never gone back and probably never will. Let me tell you why. You might have heard the name Eamon de Valera. He was our president, Ireland's president, and my commander in chief for a time. He came to this country in, I think, about 1930. And all the guys who'd fought in the IRA, and who lived in the different cities of this country, tried to meet him. I did meet him. We were living in St. Louis at the time. He asked me to go back. I told him, impossible. I had vowed I wouldn't go back to Ireland as long as the Union Jack was allowed to fly over any part of my native land; no, because too many men that I knew died that it shouldn't fly there.

But I can tell you where I'd go if I were to visit Ireland. I'd go first to some little islands off the west coast of Ireland—the Aran Islands. That's where you'll meet the real Irish people and hear Gaelic, the real Irish language. Oh, it's beautiful there, the white sands and the beaches. The quietest place in the world.

In the evening you'll hear good music and eat good food. They have these sea birds that sleep in the crevices of the cliffs, and the natives capture them when they want to have a good feed. The birds are better than chicken. If you ever happened to visit there, you knew you were welcome, that was all.

That's where they make those wonderful woolen sweaters. In my time they had their own spinning machines and wove their own wool, pure virgin wool.

Those people were never bothered by the British. They lived on islands, see, and the British couldn't govern them. Yes, they are the real Irish; those people were always free.

12

Stranded in America

In May 1914 Josepha Rozanka Rzewska *came to America from Poland to visit her aunt in Chicago. At the end of her long journey she was shocked with the news that her aunt had died. Then, before she could return to Poland, World War I broke out, ending foreign travel and cutting off all communication with her parents. Josepha was fifteen years old—and stranded in America.*

She cried a lot in those days, but with Josepha tears are a sign of deeply felt emotion, not weakness. Before long she was making headlines in this country as a recruiter for the Polish Army fighting on the side of the Allies in Europe.

She has since spent a lifetime in service to the people of Poland and America and has received many honors for her work: the Gold Cross of Merit from the Polish Army Veterans Association, and a Medal of Merit from the Polish National Alliance. In 1976 she was one of fifty persons named to the City of Chicago Hall of Fame.

Josepha and her late husband had two children. Her son died several years ago; her daughter lives in Ohio. She also has two grandchildren and one great-grandchild—three generations born in America, Josepha notes.

For the past twenty-three years she has been the librarian at the Polish National Alliance. The library is her pride and joy.

There she has put together a priceless collection of coins, rare books, artworks, medals, photographs, and other memorabilia. And once a week she meets in the library with a Red Cross unit of retired Polish-American women that she has organized.

Josepha Rzewska is a gutsy lady. She says that in her youth she was "a fireworks." She still is.

I was born in 1899 on St. Patrick's Day, March 17, in the city of Nowy-Targ, Poland. I was a seven-month baby. My mother had heard that Franz Joseph, the Austrian king, was going to go through our town on his way to see the Tatra Mountains. He was traveling in an electric car. My mother wanted to see him; so she took the horse and buggy and parked along the roadside. When the king passed, he blew the horn on his car; my mother's horse got frightened and started to run. My mother fell out of the carriage, and I was born—in a ditch beside the road. So I am a child who always travels, because I started life in travel.

I was very small. And where I come from, you have temperatures 25 and 30 degrees below zero in winter. They didn't have heaters in those days. They used to put me—I was so small—in a basket on top of the stove, you know, so that I would keep warm.

Nowy-Targ is an ancient city, a historic city. We have a church that was built by King Casimir the Great in the 1700s; it's still standing. Nowy means "new," and Targ means "mart" or "market." So the name of the town means "new market." It's located at the foot of the Tatra Mountains. When I was a little girl, every morning I used to always look out at those mountains. I loved to look at them, especially when the fog was covering the bottom and the sun was shining on the top. The colors were so beautiful. Oh, it's something that I never will forget.

Sometimes I used to get up very early in the morning, five o'clock or so, and run from our house to a forest nearby, a little over a mile away. It was a pine forest, you know, and the smell was wonderful. I liked to ride my horse—her name was Sophie—there, too.

My family had an estate in the country. We had a cottage where the people stayed who looked after the estate. I come from a family of twelve children, and each one of my brothers and sisters, when they came to a certain age, would spend one year managing the estate so that they would learn all about it. I spent a year doing that. I was fourteen—just before I came to this country. My brother was going to Krakow to finish the university, and my sister was also in college. So I said I'd go.

I managed it, and I got compliments from my mother and father about how nice I did it. I had to get up early in the morning and go to see that the servants would take care of the milk. Like everyone, you know, they might have poor relatives, and if somebody wasn't there, they might give the milk away. Of course, many times I gave it away, too. I felt sorry. And my mother—sometimes she would tell me to take a basket of food to some family. "The man is not working, and the kids are probably hungry," she'd say. "Here, take this to them." I remembered that.

My mother lost her mother, father, brothers, and sisters when she was only five years old. They died when the cholera, that terrible sickness, was in Europe. People were dying right and left, and our town was abandoned for months—not even trains came through. It was just left a dying town. My grandfather gave the land, and the people built with their hands a chapel. They built the chapel to God, praying that He would stop the cholera. The Communists have taken over my family's land, and it has been built up, but the chapel is still there. It was built in the 1850s. I was there in 1968, and I kneeled down in it. My grandfather and grandmother were the last ones buried there during the cholera.

My mother was very intelligent. She knew Polish, French, and German to read and write; and she spoke Hungarian, Ukrainian, and Czech. She was a very dedicated woman—to children and to home—but a thoroughbred Polish woman. She brought up us children to know the history of Poland, and the oppression. Whatever I am, I owe to my mother, because she was the one that taught me to help others and to want a free Poland.

My father was a builder of bridges, churches, big houses. He was the builder, and a Mr. Gunther, a German man who had settled in Poland, was the architect. My father had laborers that worked for him, and apprentices. He was the boss. But if they did something wrong, he wasn't ashamed to get in there and show them how to do it. Our family was upper middle-class. They used to say we were the richest family in town, but I don't know. Father and mother didn't spoil us. My mother taught us how to sew, how to crochet, how to knit. It helped me during the depression. I used to make out of my husband's suit myself a suit; and from the lower part of the pants, I made my son pants. I made sweaters; I made coats—and my children were always dressed.

When I was leaving for this country, my father kissed me

and coddled me and said, "You remember, nobody did anything wrong in our family. Don't be the first one. Please—that's the only blessing I can give you." And sometimes, you know, in tight corners, I could hear in my ears what Father said. I was, at a very young age, having to make the decisions of an adult. I didn't have anyone to tell me what was right and what was wrong. I was only fifteen, and I was alone in this country.

I don't think my father would have let me come if it hadn't been for my aunt. She had lost her two children when the tour boat *Eastland* sank in the Chicago River. More than 800 people, including her children, were drowned. And then her husband died. She didn't want to go back to Poland because she didn't want to leave the graves. She was all alone, and she wanted somebody to be with her. I was always, you know, the one who wanted to travel. So my father let me go.

A lady from my town in Poland was traveling to the United States. She was going to Minnesota. She was much older than I, and Father put me under her wing. She was with me on the whole trip from Nowy-Targ to Chicago. We came in 1914. But at the train station in Chicago her train was late, and she put me in a cab to go to my aunt. When I got to my aunt's house, I found out she was dead. She had died during my trip.

A friend of my aunt's, a woman who lived a couple of doors away, took me in. She helped me get in touch with my father in Poland, and he sent me money to come home. I stayed with her for a while, and then I went on to New York. I was supposed to take a ship back to Poland. But it was just the beginning of the First World War, and there was trouble with the ship. They wouldn't guarantee it. So I thought that since my father had spent so much money to send me to America, I would stay a little longer and see something of the country. The ship I was supposed to take was the *Lusitania.* It was torpedoed later by German submarines, and over a hundred American passengers were killed. After that there was no other ship going anywhere. And I lost contact completely with my family. I was left in this country all alone. I used to cry nights. Cry and cry.

I really didn't have anybody to stay with. But I was on a train heading back to Chicago, and I met a Jewish lady with two children, twins. They started screaming bloody murder, you know, and I took one of the children and put her on my lap. I started singing Polish songs to her. The mother asked me what town I came from in Poland. And I says, "Nowy-Targ."

And she says, "Oh, my goodness, my husband is from Nowy-Targ." She said his name was Raibshcid.

"Raibshcid, the family that had the bakery in the Rozanski building?" It was a building my family owned.

"Yes," she says. "How do you know?"

I says, "Because I knew your husband." I was just about four or five years old when he left. He ran away so he didn't have to go into the army. He came over here and settled in Erie, Pennsylvania.

She says, "Well, you haven't got anybody over here; come with me. My husband will be so glad. He worries about his mother. She's still in Poland. Please come and please come."

Well, I took a chance and went with her. I stayed almost two years with them. They sent me to school, and after school I helped them at their bakery. But I grew over here, inside of six months, four inches—the climate was warmer, see. I was filling out as a young lady, you know. I was then seventeen. She had a boy that was older than I, and I suppose he was looking at me and eyeing me, and so on. She noticed it, but I didn't. And one day she took me into the bedroom and told me, "You're Polish, and I have a son older than you, and I see that he is interested in you. We're Jewish people, and it would be a crisis if he married a *goy,* a gentile." She says she knows a priest, and she would ask him to try to find a place for me to live.

And so I went to live with another family. I was working in a sewing factory, the Mentor Knitting Mills. Later I became involved in the Falconnettes, a Polish youth group. I was president. At first, we were producing plays to make money for the Polish Volunteer Army, an army fighting on the side of the Allies for Poland's freedom in World War I. And then they heard me speak—found out that I was a good speaker— and Dr. Starzynski, president of the Falcons, the Polish adult organization, asked me to be a recruiter for the Polish Army.

I was recruiting officer for Massachusetts, Rhode Island, and part of Manchester, New Hampshire, and I was traveling around from place to place making speeches. That was from 1916 and 1917 until the war ended. We were working with the U.S. secretary of war in recruiting Polish-American boys for the Polish Army fighting in France. Some of the newspapers called me the best speaker in America, and I was only a half-pint.

All this time I was trying so hard to contact my mother and father in Poland. I used to send letters through friends to Sweden to a Polish priest. He would send the letters on to

Poland. And my mother was sending me letters the same way. So for a while I was getting at least three letters a year. Those were the trying days.

After the war was over, I wanted to go back to Poland, but my mother said no. She said, "Everything is torn down, here at home, and you're used to a different life; so stay until I tell you to come home." I settled in Detroit. I was working as a bookkeeper for a bakery about three years, and then I worked for the *Polish Daily Record.* I was independent. I had a cat, a dog, a canary, a Polly parrot that used to speak Polish and English, and a white rat named Dickie. I was lonesome, you know. I wanted something living to talk to, something to play around with and so forth. I killed my time that way. I didn't have to cry.

When the Polish boys, those who were from the States, started coming back to the United States after the war, I was going from hospital to hospital to visit them. Some of them didn't have anybody, just like me; they came to Golden America to make a test of it. I'd take cigarettes, take oranges, whatever I could. I felt that, as a recruiter, I took, from under a mother's breast, the boy, and sent him to war, and now he's suffering. And I helped to organize the Polish Army Veterans Ladies' Auxiliary afterwards.

I didn't want to marry when I was seventeen and eighteen; I always figured I would go back home. But then I started going with a boy that I had recruited and who had come back wounded. We got married, and when I was pregnant with my first child, my mother wrote that she was ailing. My doctor wouldn't allow me to travel because I was pregnant. I had it all prepared to go. My boy was born on the sixth of June, but on the second of July my mother passed away. I got a telegram. And then I didn't want to go.

My husband and I did go back to Poland in 1929, and we thought we would stay. General Motors appointed my husband to work for them in Warsaw. But everyone thought that Poland would join Germany in a war against Russia. It never happened, but General Motors decided not to build a factory in Poland. I wanted to stay anyway, but I thought, "My children are born in America, and there's always trouble in Poland." Poland is a football between Germany and Russia. I thought my children might one day blame me if I took them to Poland. We came back to the United States, and while we were on the ocean, we heard that we had lost our savings in the depression.

Now there isn't such poverty, but during the depression in this country, lots of people were hungry. But you never saw the Polish people going to the bread lines; they were too proud to go to get something for nothing. So I would ask some of the families to come to have dinner with me. I didn't have much, but I always shared it.

It was later, in 1948, that I was asked to work for a month with the National Catholic Welfare Conference to set up a resettlement program for displaced Polish people. These were Polish men and their families who had fought against Russia during the Second World War. They couldn't go back to Poland because the Russians would kill them. The United States Congress had passed an act to permit so many from different countries in Europe to settle in this country. My office brought close to 50,000 Polish people to America—close to 25,000 to Chicago. I was processing papers, and I had to find sponsors for these people. So I went from one society to another and I spoke. They needed people to give them a home for a couple of days, somebody to give them a start. The month stretched into years—until 1953.

Even today, whenever I meet somebody that came through resettlement, they come and kiss me all over. They would do anything for me—they are so thankful that they could come to America. They're good Americans, but they're good Polish people, too. They appreciate their heritage.

I think it's amazing that we have Germans, Slavs, Russians, Italians, English, Irish—everybody—in America. And we all work together. We don't fight and have wars. Why can't they do that in Europe? In Europe they're always fighting. I have some Jewish people, good friends; I have Italian people, very good friends. Living next door to me, Germans, and we are the best of friends.

I'm the only one from my family living in this country. Five of my sisters are living still in Poland. And they're well off—they all have businesses. Most are furriers. You know, so many sheep are raised in the mountains, and my sisters buy the skins and make coats out of them.

One time, when I was a little girl about ten years old, an artist, a friend of my family, was painting my portrait, and he was talking to me. He asked me, "What do you intend to do when you grow up?" And I answered him that I wanted to travel, see what's what, how different people live in the world. And then, when I was finished, I wanted to come back to my beautiful hills, the Tatra Mountains. Only part of my wish came true.

Suggested Reading List

Acuna, Rodolfo. *Occupied America: The Chicano's Struggle Toward Liberation.* San Francisco: Canfield Press, 1972. Paperback.

Amfitheatrof, Erik. *The Children of Columbus.* Boston: Little, Brown and Company, 1973.

Coles, Robert. *The Old Ones of New Mexico.* Albuquerque: University of New Mexico Press, 1973.

Conrat, Maisie & Richard. *Executive Order 9066: The Internment of 110,000 Japanese-Americans.* Cambridge, Mass.: The M.I.T. Press, 1972. Paperback.

Erickson, Charlotte. *Invisible Immigrants: The Adaptation of English and Scottish Immigrants in Nineteenth-Century America.* Coral Gables, Fla.: University of Miami Press, 1972.

Gambino, Richard. *Blood of My Blood.* New York: Doubleday & Company, Inc., 1974. Paperback.

Glazer, Nathan, and Moynihan, Daniel P. *Beyond the Melting Pot.* 2nd ed. Cambridge, Mass.: The M.I.T. Press, 1970. Paperback.

Handlin, Oscar. *The Uprooted.* 2nd ed. Boston: Little, Brown and Company, 1973. Paperback.

Howe, Irving. *World of Our Fathers: The Journey of East European Jews to America and the Life They Found and Made.* New York: Harcourt Brace Jovanovich, Inc., 1976.

Jones, Maldwyn A. *American Immigration*. Chicago: University of Chicago Press, 1960.

―――. *Destination America*. New York: Holt, Rinehart and Winston, 1976.

Meier, Matt S., and Rivera, Feliciano. *The Chicanos: A History of Mexican Americans*. New York: Hill & Wang, 1972.

Nelli, Humbert S. *The Italians in Chicago 1880-1930*. New York: Oxford University Press, Inc., 1973.

O'Connor, Richard. *The German-Americans: An Informal History*. Boston: Little, Brown and Company, 1968.

Potter, George W. *To the Golden Door: The Story of the Irish in Ireland and America*. Reprint. Westport, Conn.: Greenwood Press, Inc., 1974.

Shannon, William V. *The American Irish: A Political and Social Portrait*. expanded ed. New York: Collier Books, 1974. Paperback.

Sung, B.L. *The Story of the Chinese in America*. New York: Collier Books, 1971. Paperback. This book is available in hardcover under the title *Mountain of Gold*. New York: Macmillan, Inc., 1967.

Weglyn, Michi. *Years of Infamy: The Untold Story of America's Concentration Camps*. New York: William Morrow & Co., Inc., 1976.

Wittke, Carl F. *We Who Built America: The Saga of the Immigrant*. rev. ed. Cleveland: Press of Case-Western Reserve University, 1967.

Wytrwal, Joseph A. *America's Polish Heritage: A Social History of the Poles in America*. Detroit: Endurance Press, 1961.